DEFENDING THE PAPACY

Gerard Morrissey

CHRISTENDOM PUBLICATIONS
Crossroads Books
Route 3, Box 87
Front Royal, Virginia 22630

L.C. Classification Number: BX1753.M677
ISBN: 0-931888-15-8

CONTENTS

The publication of this book was made possible in part through the support of the Christendom Publishing Group. Members are listed below:

Anonymous
Anonymous
Anonymous
Mrs. Marie Barrett
Mr. Daniel Bauer
LCDR C. W. Baumann
Mr. & Mrs. John and Opal Baye
Mr. Joseph C. Berzanskis
Mr. Joe Bierek
Mr. A. J. Birdsell
Mr. & Mrs. Joseph C. Bowling
Mr. John F. Bradley
Reverend Nicholas Brennan
Mr. George Bridgman
Mr. & Mrs. Robert Brindle
Mrs. Martha Brown
Mr. James G. Bruen Jr.
Deacon Patrick Bruen
Mrs. Robert C. Bryant
Mrs. Edith L. Buckley
Mr. Doyle G. Burke
Mr. & Mrs. Merv Burns
Paul A. Busam M.D.
Mrs. Marie Butkus
Mrs. Margaret Buytaert
Mr. Thomas J. Calvo
Mr. Charles M. Campbell
Miss Priscilla Carmody
Joseph C. Cascarelli Esq.
Rev. Francis A. Cegielka SAC
Mrs. Virginia J. Chipp
Mr. Eugene V. Clark
Mr. & Mrs. Christopher Colclough
Mrs. S. J. Conner
Rev. Edward J. Connolly
Mr. John W.W. Cooper
Msgr. Henry Cosgrove
Mr. Terence J. Coyne
CH (Maj) Alfred M. Croke
Mr. & Mrs. Chris N. Cuddeback
Reverend John J. Cusack
Mr. Robert J. Cynkar
Mrs. Ellen L. Dalby
Sister M. Damian
The Dateno Family
Mr. B. P. Davidson
Mrs. George de Lorimier
Mr. William De Lozier

Mrs. Jack Deardurff
Reverend Herman J. Deimel
Reverend Robert J. Dempsey
Dr. Joseph L. DeStefano
Mrs. Mary L. Dix
Reverend Daniel B. Dixon
Mr. Thomas C. Domeika
Mr. & Mrs. Leon W. Doty
Mr. Thomas J. Dowdall
Mr. Edward A. Dreis
Mr. D. J. Duckworth
Mr. John H. Duffy
Reverend J. A. Duraczynski
Mrs. James Ebben
Mrs. Clarence Ebert
Mr. D. N. Ehart
Mr. Clinton M. Elges
Sister Ellen, S.J.W.
Mr. William W. Elliott
Mrs. Betty Emilio
Reverend George S. Endal S.J.
Mrs. Frances A. Esfeld
Mr. Francis G. Fanning
Mr. & Mrs. Victor Fernandez
Mrs. Gilda Fidell
Mr. & Mrs. James G. Fischer
Miss Margaret C. Fitzgerald
G. F. Flagg Family
Mr. Emmet Flood
Mr. Eugene P. Foeckler Sr.
Mr. John F, Foell
Mrs. Donald B. Fox M.D.
Mr. & Mrs. J. P. Frank Jr.
Mrs. Claudette Fredricksen
Mrs. Adele Fricke
Mr. Martin Froeschl
Mr. Eduardo Garcia-Ferrer
Mr. & Mrs. John Gardner
Mr. Edward Patrick Garrigan
Mrs. Shirley Gasquet
Mr. Richard L. Gerhards
Msgt. R. P. Gideon
Mr. Carl J. Graham
Cpt & Mrs. James P. Guerrero
Mr. Patrick Guinan
Mrs. Paula Haigh
Reverend A. A. Halbach
Mr. Robert E. Hanna

Mrs. Mary J. Hart
Mrs. Mary T. Hatfield
Mr. Frank E. Hauck
Mr. David Havlicek
Reverend Brian J. Hawker
Mrs. Francis Heaverlo
Reverend Herman L. Heide
Reverend Hugh P. Henneberry S.S.J.
Reverend Albert J. Herbert S.M.
Mrs. W. Herbert
Mr. Ronald H. Herrmann
Mr. larry L. Hobbs
Mr. Joseph L. Holtz
Arthur Hopkins M.D.
Mr. John C. Horan
Mr. & Mrs. Andre Huck
Mrs. Doris L. Huff
Edgar Hull M.D.
Mrs. Carmen Iacobelli
Reverend Jeffrey A. Ingham
Ms. Mildred M. Jackson
Mr. Herman Jadloski
Mr. J. Janeski
Mr. & Mrs. Dave Jaszkowiak
Mrs. Kathleen C. Jones
Mr. Marley Francis Jones
Mr. Daniel P. Judge
Mr. Edward E. Judge
Rev. Matthew S. Kafka
Mr. & Mrs. Albert Kais
Mrs. J. M. Keiper
Miss Betty Kelly
Reverend Michael J. Kelly
Mr. & Mrs. Frank Knoell
Mr. John R. Knoll
Mr. Augustine Kofler
Mr. William C. Koneazny
Dr. Edward J. Krol
James W. Lassiter M.D.
Miss Therese Lawrence
Mr. Edward A. Lewandowski
Reverend Harry J. Lewis
Very Rev. Victor O. Lorenz
Mr. William J. Lucas
Mrs. Jan Lundberg
Mrs. Carolyn C. MacDonald
Miss Katherine I. MacDonald
Mr. George F. Manhardt
Mr. Thomas Manning
Miss Jeanette Maschmann
N. Anthony Mastropietro M.D.
Mr. Thomas J. May

Reverend Mark G. Mazza
Mrs. Verlie McArdle
Mr. Steven McCallan
Mr. Thomas J. McCann
Mr. W. C. McCarthy
Reverend William R. McCarthy
Mr. John A. McCarty Esq.
Mr. James McConnell
Mr. Robert McConville
Mrs. Miriam McCue
Robert E. McCullough M.D.
Mr. Joseph D. McDaid
Mr. & Mrs. Dennis P. McEneany
Reverend P. J. McHugh
Mr. Thomas A. McLaughlin
Mr. J. R. McMahon
Mr. Robert Cruise McManus
Mrs. Kenneth McNichol
Reverend Edward J. Melvin C.M.
Patrick A. Metress
Mr. Larry G. Miezio
Mr. & Mrs. Larry Miggins
Mrs. Robert L. Miller
Mr. Michael P. Millner
Mr. Joseph Monahan
Reverend Hugh Monmonier
Mr. James B. Mooney
Mrs. Gertrude G. Moore
Miss A. Morelli
Col. Chester H. Morneau
Mr. Nicholas J. Mulhall
Joseph P. Mullally Ph.D.
Mr. & Mrs. G. W. Muth
Mrs. Marie Mutz
Mr. Frank C. Nelick
Mr. L. J. Netzel
Mr. Frank Newlin
Mr. Joseph F. O'Brien
Reverend Philip O'Donnell
Mr. & Mrs. Tim O'Donnell
Mr. John F. O'Shaughnessy Jr.
Mr. Lawrence P. O'Shaughnessy
Mrs. Josephine K. Olmstead
Mrs. Veronica M. Oravec
Mrs. John F. Parker
Mr. Ernest Patry
Reverend Angelo Patti
Brother Stephen F. Paul
Reverend Laszlo Pavel
Mr. & Mrs. Joseph and Mary Peek
Bill and Mary Peffley
Mr. Alfred H. Pekarek

Robert N. Pelaez M.D.
Mr. & Mrs. Gerald R. Pfeiffer
Mr. & Mrs. Pat Pollock
Mr. Frank Poncelet
Mr. & Mrs. William H. Power Jr.
Dr. & Mrs. C. Pruzzia
Mr. E. K. Quickenton
Mr. Stuart Quinlan
Mrs. Mary F. Quinn
Mr. Thomas J. Quinn
Dr. William E. Rabil
Miss Beatrice A. Rappengluck
Mr. & Mrs. Joseph E. Rau
Reverend Robert A. Reed
Dr. & Mrs. Francis C. Regan
Mrs. John F. Reid
Mr. & Mrs. John J. Reuter
Msgr. William J. Reynolds
Dr. Charles E. Rice
M. V. Rock M.D.
Brother Philip Romano OFMCap
Mrs. Mary A. Rosenast
Mrs. Paul Rosenberger
Mr. Bernard J. Ruby
Mr. Mark V. Ruessmann
Mrs. Agnes Ryan
Mr. G. Salazar
Mr. Richard W. Sassman
Mr. & Mrs. George Scanlon
Miss Marian C. Schatzman
Miss Constance M. Scheetz
Mrs. Margaret Scheetz
Mr. Peter Scheetz
Mrs. Francis R. Schirra
Mrs. Claragene Schmidt
Mrs. Job A. Schumacher
Mr. & Mrs. Ralph Schutzman
Mr. P. J. Schwirian
Mr. Frank P. Scrivener
Mr. & Mrs. Robert K. Scrivener
John B. Shea
John R. Sheehan M.D.
Miss Anne Sherman
Mr. W. R. Sherwin
Mr. & Mrs. Dale P. Siefker
Mrs. Bernice Simon
Mr. Richard M. Sinclair Jr.

Capt. Arthur Sippo
Mrs. Walter Skorupski
Mr. S. C. Sloane
Miss Mary Smerski
Mrs. Joan M. Smith
Mrs. Mary Carole Smith
Mr. William Smith
Mrs. William Smith
Mrs. Ann Spalding
Mr. & Mrs. James Spargo
Mr. & Mrs. Victor Spielman
Miss Anne M. Stinnett
Mr. Michael Sullivan
Mr. John Svarc
Mr. Edward S. Szymanski
Ms. C. G. Teixeira
Mr. Raymond F. Tesi
Reverend Clyde Tillman
Mr. Edward B. Timko
Mr. Richard J. Titus
Mr. Dominic Torlone
Rev. Chris Twohig
Mr. Michael Vachon
Mr. & Mrs. Albert Vallone
Mr. Wil Van Achthoven
Mrs. Alice Vandenberg
Reverend Frederick J. Vaughn
Mr. William C. Vinet Jr.
Mrs. Margaret Vogenbeck
Reverend George T. Voiland
Mrs. Catherine Wahlmeier
Mr. David P. Walkey
Miss Kathleen Walsh
Honorable Vernon A. Walters
Mrs. Alice V. Ward
Mr. Fulton John Waterloo
Mr. Ralph A. Wellings
Mrs. Joan Weth
Mr. J. Weusten
Mr. Alfred L. White
Miss Penny Wiest
Mr. John R. Wilhelmy
Mrs. Mary Williams
Mrs. Mary Wimmenauer
Mr. Michael C. Winn
Mrs. Marguerite A. Wright
James F. Zimmer M.D.

Introduction

This book is written in the hope that it may assist Catholics who have been disturbed by the happenings in the Catholic Church since the Second Vatican Council. Many Catholics have suffered a severe crisis of faith because of the changes that have taken place in recent years. Sadly, some of the people have already left the Church. Others remain, but they will tell you quite frankly that they feel as if the Church has abandoned them.

In addition to this group of people, there are other Catholics who can accept without difficulty those changes authorized by the Church but who are rightly upset when they see the Holy Father being ridiculed and the Church's teachings being dismissed with contempt. What is especially disturbing is that such vicious attacks often come from those within the Church itself—and, even more unsettling, from Catholics who occupy positions of some authority on the local level. For example, one may well live in a parish where a priest looks upon the teachings of the Pope with a thinly veiled contempt (if, indeed, the contempt is veiled at all). Or perhaps the problem is the diocesan newspaper, the official voice of the local church. As the Apostolic Delegate, the Pope's official representative, stated in an April 1981 letter to the American bishops:

> With increasing frequency the Holy See receives letters from the United States complaining about articles appearing in Catholic newspapers, including diocesan publications, which cause harm to the Faith of the people because of lack of respect for the teaching and decisions of the magisterium. As you know, it is not unusual for such articles to contain criticism and attacks even on the teaching authority and the person of the Holy Father. The impact of such criticism is heightened when columns are syndicated and widely circulated.

Perhaps your own faith is not shaken by these attacks on the Pope; still, you may well feel a sense of frustration and powerlessness. Perhaps you would like to defend the Pope. You would like to promote the teaching of the Church. But how? Can you actually accomplish anything?

The answer to that last question is a definite "yes." In fact, the active involvement of loyal Catholics can be crucial in restoring to the Church a sense of reverence for the teaching authority of the Pope and the Bishops.

On the other hand, those who are working so hard to tear down the authority of the Pope will continue to make advances unless sufficient numbers of Catholics who support the Pope join together in groups and work actively in support of Church teachings.

What we have just written could be put in the form of three questions.

(1) What is the official teaching of the Church?

(2) If, as the Apostolic Delegate's letter indicates, many Church institutions in the United States are undermining this teaching and harming the faith, then how in the world did the present situation develop and why have those attacking the Church from within made such progress?

(3) What steps can be taken by Catholics loyal to the Pope both to safeguard their own faith (and the faith of their children) and to strengthen respect for the Church's teaching authority within the Catholic community in our country?

Initially, it was my intention to discuss all three of these questions in the present volume, but it soon became clear that the result would be a rather lengthy book. Therefore, I have decided to focus on questions two and three in later works.

In the present volume, we will consider changes within the Church. What in the Church is permanent and can never be altered? On the other hand, what can change? The purpose here is to understand clearly that—although many things in the Church have changed since the time of the Vatican Council—the basic teachings of the Church remain.

While this can certainly be said about all of the changes that have actually taken place, it must be immediately added that those challenging the Pope often advocate the most revolutionary kind of changes in the Catholic Faith. The Divinity of Our Lord, the Resurrection of Jesus from the Dead, the Real Presence of Our Lord in the Eucharist—all these Catholic beliefs, as well as many other Church teachings, are under constant attack. In a special way, this attack involves an attempt to overthrow the teaching authority of the Pope, to convince the Catholic people to take the word of an "intellectual elite" over the word of the Pope himself when it comes to Church doctrine. Therefore, we will consider authority within the Church, the different kinds of authority, and the emphasis placed by the Second Vatican Council upon the authority of the Pope.

Before studying these questions, however, let us consider for a moment the personal suffering of many Catholics—a deep anguish caused by feelings of loneliness, doubt, and abandonment in today's Church.

1.
For Those Who Are Suffering

If you are old enough to remember things prior to 1945, you experienced a Church that in many ways was very different from the Church of the present. Some people sneer at this Church. They keep saying how wonderful it is that they no longer live in that Church of the past. But suppose you feel differently. Suppose you had a great love for that Church of the past, a love for the customs that are no longer there, and a reverence that you do not feel in today's Church.

Perhaps the devotional life of the Church no longer seems to give you the feeling of love that existed once before. Instead, you feel as if everything has been pulled away from you. Like a person who finds it difficult to breathe, you may be gasping, trying to find spiritual meaning in your life. All you know is that the Church of the past gave you that spiritual meaning. The Church of the present does not.

Perhaps—if you experience this kind of feeling—you have a temptation to act like some friends of yours. They go to what is sometimes referred to as a "traditional" church. It has the Mass the way it was before, and has many of the customs within the Church exactly the way they were before. Such a Church has a strong appeal to you. Nevertheless, you do not go, because your mind tells you that there is one thing this "traditional" church does not have. While trying to keep the external traditions of the Church, it has rejected the authority of the Pope. It has done exactly what those attacking the Church have always done.

That leaves you with a painful choice. You can have all the external traditions of the Church, all the old customs, if you attend that "traditional" church. But the price would be abandoning the Pope. So you resist the temptation. On the other hand, when you go to your local parish church, you find not the customs of the past but new customs that have absolutely no meaning for you. It all appears dry and useless.

What shall be said about this? The answer lies in considering the problem of suffering.

Personal Suffering

Let us consider Our Lord's own Life. He had moments of great honor. On Palm Sunday, the crowds were cheering Him. Everything seemed to be going wonderfully. But Palm Sunday was followed by Good Friday. The day of external triumph was followed by a time when Our Lord was alone and helpless.

Honor followed by rejection. Popularity followed by loneliness. It was this way throughout the Life of Jesus. There were days when the crowds hailed Him and sought to make Him their King. There were also occasions when they turned from Our Lord and refused to follow Him. On one such occasion, we are told that the reason so many refused to follow Christ was that He was giving them "hard sayings". He was telling them things that they did not believe and had no wish to hear. In other words, they were not really following the Lord but themselves. They would follow Jesus as long as He told them what they wanted, as long as He was a symbol of their own desires. The moment He told them what they did not want, they rejected His Authority and turned from Him.

How similar all this is to the attitude that many Catholics of today have about the Pope, the Vicar of Christ on earth! They also are determined to reject any "hard sayings." They will follow the Pope only as long as the Pope follows them and does exactly what they want.

It is not by accident that the life of the Church follows the Life of Our Lord. Like Our Lord Himself, the Church has "golden ages" when everything seems to be going well. There are times when the Church holds a respected position in society, as there were times when Our Lord Himself was popular.

At these times it is easy to follow Christ and His Church. However, there are other times as well, times when it is extremely difficult to be a Catholic, times when there appears to be nothing but the Cross—in others words, times of suffering.

Reflect upon Our Lord's own Crucifixion. A few days after He was hailed by everyone, only a handful remained with Him. With the exception of John, even the Apostles chosen by Our Lord Himself had deserted Him, just as they had fallen asleep in the Garden when He most needed their support. Our Blessed Lady, of course, never deserted Our Lord. She stood with Him under the Cross. As a Mother she loved her Son as no one else could. As a Mother she naturally wanted to reach out and help Him. Yet she had to stand by and see Him suffer terribly. She had to watch her Son die, and she was utterly powerless to do anything to stop it.

How easy it would have been for Mary to turn away and leave. Like those Catholics of today who abandon the Pope and run for comfort to "traditionalist" churches, Mary could have said: "I just can't take the frustration and the controversy any more. I have to go someplace else and look for the happiness I once had." But Mary did not leave Her Son. She stood by and accepted every suffering that came Her way, even the powerlessness, the inability to stop those who were torturing Her Son right in front of her eyes. Ironically, it was in this moment of apparent uselessness that—through God's grace—Mary was actually most powerful because her faith and love perfectly fulfilled God's plan for her. She was fully united with her Son Who was redeeming the world at the very time when He seemed to be undergoing a final defeat.

Should we not meditate constantly upon the suffering of Our Lord and our Blessed Lady? Any suffering we endure, they endured to a far greater extent. If we feel lonely in today's Church, we must consider how lonely they felt on Calvary.

If the past was a peaceful time for us while the present is like a desert, if the present is full of difficulties while the past was full of joy, then it is only natural for us to look back on the past as a "golden age" and to sorrow over the present. Nevertheless, we should also realize that in our present sorrow we can in our own lives relive Our Lord's Crucifixion. The most important gift we can offer to Jesus is to stay within His Church and bear up under our present suffering. It is good and wonderful that we felt a feeling of love and joy when we went to Church in the past. If at present we feel nothing and continue to attend Mass only because we believe this is what Christ would wish, that very act can be even more valuable precisely because we have no rewards in terms of personal feeling. We act out of the same love that Christ had when He chose to accept the suffering of the Cross in order to be faithful to His Mission.

In addition to what has already been said, there is something else that should be understood by Catholics who no longer have the feeling of religion in today's Church that they had in the past. Feelings come and go. This does not mean that feelings are unimportant. It does not mean that we should not hope to have a feeling of religion. What it does mean is that if for some reason we do not have these feelings, we have in no way lost our religion. Although we may feel nothing, our relationship with Our Lord can be (if we cooperate with God's Grace) even closer than before. All that we have lost is the emotional satisfaction that we used to have.

For example, consider marriage. When two people give themselves to each other in marriage, they usually experience what is referred to as "a honeymoon period". They have strong feelings of love and devotion for each other. The feelings are so powerful that they overwhelm everything else. Problems appear to be non-existent. Yet this honeymoon period passes in time. No longer do the married couple feel the same deep emotions that they experienced in the past. Problems may now begin to surface. It is more difficult for the married couple to live their relationship with each other than it was during the honeymoon period. What they once were able to do with ease they now have to struggle for.

Does this mean that they have lost their love for each other? Not at all. What they have lost is the strong emotional feeling that made everything so easy. It is only natural to regret that loss. All of us would much prefer strong feelings of joy and love to no feeling at all, or perhaps to negative feelings of discouragement. However, it is vital not to identify love with the feeling of love. Love in a marriage is the willingness to give oneself to the other person and this love can sometimes be even greater when there is no feeling at all. Perhaps it could be put this way. When the feeling of love goes, then the love that a man and woman have for each other will be tested—because the feeling is no longer there to make it easy for them to give themselves to each other.

We can see the same difference between love and feeling when we look at a mother and her child. After a baby is born, there is a great feeling of happiness. But suppose the months have passed. Now the baby is sick. To help her baby, the mother must get up eight or ten times in the middle of the night. The child keeps crying out. What does the mother feel at this time? She certainly does not experience that great emotion of love that thrilled her when she first held her baby in her arms. To be frank, what she probably experiences is a feeling of exhaustion. "Here we go again" might describe her emotional reaction when she hears her baby crying. In fact, her feelings would tell her to stay in bed and go back to sleep. What is it that motivates the mother to get up and help her child? It is her love, her determination to reach out and to do whatever she can to help her baby. It is this love that makes her act against her feelings which tell her to remain in bed. At this moment, the mother may well love her baby even more than she did when she first held that baby in her arms because she is now acting out of love, against her feeling, while in the joyful times her feelings made it easy for her to love.

The test of love is what we do when we must sacrifice in order to follow that love. As the test of a love of a man and woman for each other comes in moments of sacrifice—as the test of a mother's love for her child comes in moments of sacrifice—so the test of our love for Christ and for His Church comes in moments when we must sacrifice.

Please keep this in mind if you are among those people who do not have the feeling of love and devotion in today's Church that you had in the past. It is only natural for you to hope that the time of sacrifice will pass and that the feeling of joy will return, just as the mother naturally hopes that the time of having to get up in the middle of the night will pass and that her child's health will return. Nevertheless, you should also realize that this period of emotional dryness can be an opportunity to show your love for Our Lord in a very special way.

A marriage sometimes falls apart when the feeling of love leaves. Although the married couple may not have been aware of it, they were actually in love with the feeling rather than in love with each other. Thus, when the "romance" disappears, there is nothing left. Or perhaps they "fall in love" with someone else. The phrase "fall in love" can often refer not to true love but to romantic feeling. In that sense, people can fall in love with somebody they have only met for an instant. They are in love with the feeling rather than in love with the person.

In the same way, we must ask ourselves this question: Are we in love with God? Or, when we practice our religion, are we in love with the religious feeling that we experience? If we are primarily in love with the feeling, then we may well drift away from the Catholic Church if ever that feeling disappears. We may go someplace else in search of that "old religious feeling"—like a husband who leaves his wife for some other woman with whom he can experience that "old romantic feeling".

On the other hand, if our religion is based primarily on love and not on feeling, on what we believe God has actually done for us in Christ, on something that is and always will be true regardless of the presence or absence of "religious feeling" on our part, then we will stay with Christ and His Church, not only on Palm Sunday but also on Good Friday.

Doubt

Having considered both suffering and the difference between religion and feeling, let us turn to the problem of doubt.

One suffering that many people have in today's Church is a feeling of doubt. In the past they were certain of their religion. Now, either becuase of the changes or because of the attacks upon the Church, they experience moments of uncertainty and doubt. Is it all true? Or is it perhaps only a dream to believe that Christ saved us?

As with Our Lord's own Life, as with our discussion of suffering, we should recognize that there are periods of life when faith comes easily and there are other times when it is very difficult to believe. What we wrote about suffering applies also to doubt, which is, after all, a form of suffering.

What should you do if you are troubled by doubt? First—and most important—you should pray. Ask God for His Help and His assistance. Perhaps the doubt may trouble you so much that you find it difficult to concentrate on prayer. If you cannot pray as you normally would, then offer this very inability up as a suffering to Our Lord. Ask Jesus and Mary to help you to pray.

Second, you should seek help from others. As in all forms of suffering, the support of other people can be vital to us. Put yourself in contact with Catholics who love their faith. Their help and their support will assist you in any crisis. Do not hesitate to talk to a priest but be sure the priest is one who has loyalty to the Pope and to the teaching authority of the Church rather than a person who might further undermine your faith by rejecting the Church's teaching.

Finally, it is important to remember that doubt does not imply in any way that you have done anything wrong or that your faith has been lost. There is a famous saying that 10,000 difficulties do not make a single doubt. In other words, there is a crucial difference between temptation and sin. We may be tempted many times, but the very temptation can be a source of grace for us. Sin only occurs when we consciously accept the temptation, when we choose something wrong with what the Church refers to as sufficient reflection and full consent of the will.

Therefore, when we say that 10,000 difficulties do not make a single doubt, we are saying that 10,000 temptations do not make a single sin. We are using the word "doubt" to refer to a conscious decision not to believe, and the word "difficulty" to refer to those temptations which may make it very hard for us to believe.

God will not abandon us if we wish to remain faithful to Him. The only thing that can separate us from the Lord is our conscious decision to reject Him. So if you are faced with doubt, then recognize that this is simply a temptation. While it may be a most anguishing experience, remember that some of the greatest saints in the Church also suffered in this way. They kept their faith by prayer and by seeking the help of others. If you take the same steps, you too can be strengthened in your relationship with Our Lord.

2.
What Can Change
and What Cannot

Suppose that you are walking down the street. You meet a friend, Sally Smith, whom you have not seen in many years. You ask Sally how she's doing, and she replies: "Well, I've made a number of changes in my life. For one thing, I changed my hat. You know that old hat I wore for years. Well, now I have a new one. In addition, I changed my house, moved 40 miles away. Finally, I also changed my husband. I'm no longer Sally Smith—now I'm Sally Jones".

Having heard all that, you express surprise at that last change, the change of husband. Sally responds: "If you accept the other changes, why are you surprised at that one? After all, if you think about it, I've worn that old hat and lived in that old house even longer than I was married to my husband."

I think we would instinctively reply: "Sally, that's not the point. There's a big, big difference between changing your hat, changing your house, and changing your husband."

In other words, time is not the only factor. The principal consideration is the importance of what is involved. A family can change their place of residence and still be the same family. A family can change a great many other customs and still be the same family. On the other hand, if Mrs. Smith changes her husband and marries someone else, then you no longer have the same family. (In fact, that is signified by her change of name from Mrs. Smith to Mrs. Jones.)

What is true of a family is also true of the Church. Some things in the Church, even while they may be very old, are basically customs or Church (rather than divine) laws. These elements can be changed. That does not mean that they ought to be changed. In fact, we may feel rather strongly that they should not. But it does mean that they are capable of being changed. Other elements of the Church's life, come from God (divine law, the teachings of Christ). They are essential to the Church and cannot be changed—no more than a family could change the husband and still remain the same family.

What are some of these basic beliefs that cannot change? While the following summary does not include everything, it does cover many fundamental Catholic beliefs (and not one of these beliefs has been changed).

Basic Teachings

God is a Person Who knows us and loves us. We are made for God—that is, the purpose of our life is to make a journey to God. At the end of our life on earth, we hope to be completely united with God in heaven. (In this world, we do not have this complete unity, which is the reason that we often feel that something is missing, as if we were separated from someone. But even in this life, through faith and love, we know God in part.)

During our earthly journey, we try to develop ourselves as persons in preparation for meeting God. We do this especially by loving God and by loving those other people whom we come across in our life. All the things that happen to us—even the crises, the tragedies, the sufferings that are apparently meaningless—we can use as occasions for giving ourselves more fully.

Not only does God love us but He has revealed Himself to us. Throughout human history men have tried to reach God. Catholics believe that God does not stand by passively: He, too, has been active; He has reached out to men, entering our lives.

In the Bible, the Inspired Word of God, we read of the way in which God manifested Himself to Abraham, to Moses, to David, and to the other great religious figures of the Old Testament. And then, in what St. Paul refers to as the "appointed times", God gave us the greatest gift of all, His Son, Jesus Christ, conceived by the power of the Holy Spirit and born of the Virgin Mary.

Our Lord Jesus Christ is both God and Man. As God, He is the Second Person of the Blessed Trinity. As Man, He is the "new Adam" who redeemed us by His Life, Death, Resurrection, and Ascension.

By original sin, the sin of Adam, we were cut off from the union we were destined to have with God. The Church has compared us to the deaf and dumb man cured by Our Lord. If we came upon a deaf man, we would not think it was his fault. Nevertheless, the illness does keep him from communicating with others as he should. In the same way, original sin, while not our fault, keeps us from spiritually communicating with God as we should. By His Life, Death, Resurrection, and Ascension, Jesus restored our life with God. Men, who were cut off, could not reach God, but God could, and did, reach out to men.

In taking on a human nature, God the Son truly becomes one of us. The One Person is both God and Man. St. Paul reminds us that, as Man, Christ is like us in all ways except for sin. Our Lord, therefore, could experience both joys and sorrows. We see that He had friends, a family life (one of the great Catholic devotions is imitating Christ in His Love for His Mother), emotions. He could experience all the sufferings we do—and, in fact, He did in His Passion: the physical sufferings—torture, thirst, crucifixion, scourging—the feeling of loneliness, and of fear in the Garden, desertion by His friends, betrayal by one of them, failure on the human level, the irony of being charged with not loving His father—he was the object of ridicule, the victim of unjust persecution.

In His Death, Christ gave up His human life to God for us. He passed over to His Father, making the journey to God for us. (The Church recalls the Old Testament Exodus, the Jewish people going out from Egypt into the desert, because of their belief in a promised land, a land they had never seen. Jesus reveals that what happened to them physically is the story of our journey through life. We pass out of this life, through death, into the land God has promised, a land we do not see but must believe in, as the Jews believed in their promised land. So the Christian theology of death tells us that death is not the end of our journey, any more than the desert was the end of the journey for the Jewish people. Through death life is changed, not taken away, and, even as we sorrow over the end of this life, we look forward in hope to our future life with God.) In the Resurrection, God the Father showed His acceptance of Christ's Offering. In the Ascension, Jesus returns to His Father.

The Church, through the Mass and Sacraments, bring us into contact with Christ's Life, so that our lives, yet to experience death, resurrection, and ascension, are joined with His.

During His lifetime on earth, Our Lord chose Apostles and trained them to carry on His mission. Prior to His Ascension, He promised to be with them always and to send the Holy Spirit, the Third Person of the Blessed Trinity. On Pentecost—the "Birthday of the Church"—the Holy Spirit came upon the Apostles who were gathered together around Mary, the Mother of the Lord.

Of the Apostles, Peter was chosen in a special way to be the "rock" upon which the Church was to be built. The Bishops in the Church today are successors of the Apostles and the Pope is the successor of St. Peter. As successors of Peter and the Apostles, the Pope and the Bishops united with him have been given authority by Our Lord to teach, govern and sanctify His Church.

At the heart of the Church today and always is the Sacrifice of the Mass which is a memorial both of Christ's Last Supper with His Disciples and of His Death on the Cross. However, the Mass is not only a memorial of the past but an action of Christ in the present that looks forward to the future, the Church's eventual complete reunion with the Lord. In the Mass, Jesus Christ again offers Himself to His Father and the Bread and Wine consecrated by the priest at the Mass literally become—as Our Lord Himself stated at the Last Supper—the Body and the Blood of the Lord. The followers of Christ receive Our Lord in Holy Communion and, in turn, pledge themselves to Him.

Christ has given to the Church seven sacraments—outward signs instituted by the Lord to give grace. These seven sacraments are expressions of Our Lord's love for us at the most important moments of our lives, and ways to express our love for Him. Through one sacrament, Baptism, the Divine Life first comes to us and we are initiated into the Church. Through another, Confirmation, we are strengthened by the Holy Spirit as were the Apostles at Pentecost. There is a sacrament for the physically sick (Anointing), and a sacrament for the spiritually sick who wish to seek God's forgiveness for their sins (Penance). There is a sacrament for two Christians who wish to consecrate themselves to each other in Matrimony and form a family in the Lord, and there is a Sacrament of Orders by which Bishops are consecrated as successors of the Apostles and priests are ordained to assist the Bishops. Most important of all, there is the Sacrament of the Eucharist—the Sacrament of Our Lord's Body and Blood.

Christ comes to us, of course, in many ways outside of the seven sacraments. For instance, Our Lord comes to us when we pray and Catholics are encouraged to pray both by themselves and in groups and to offer up their work and suffering to the Lord. Through God's Grace, each of us may be given a role as a Christian missionary in bringing the love of God to some other person. We may do this personally to those around us or, through our prayers and sufferings, we may be of assistance to people whom we may never meet. We believe that this Christian union extends even beyond the grave: we can be helped by the saints in heaven and our own prayers can assist those who have died in the state of grace but who may not as yet be fully united with the Lord.

Although everyone in heaven is a saint, the Church on earth chooses certain individuals whom it holds up to us as models. The Church encourages us to select some of these saints and to pray to them for assistance in our life. Of all the saints united with Our Lord, the first and foremost is His Blessed Mother, who is not only the Mother of God but our spiritual mother and the mother of the entire Church. Catholics are urged to pray to Mary in a special way and to give the Mother of Jesus a prominent place in their devotional life.

God has not promised us that we will have all the goods of this life, although we are encouraged to pray for legitimate desires. But one promise God has made to us: eventually, we will be united with Him. There is only one thing that can prevent this union—a free and conscious decision on our part to turn away from the Lord by serious sin. Because we have free will, we do retain the possibility of abandoning Christ all of our life. However, this is not something that happens to us from without but something we must consciously choose. Therefore, we can be confident that—if we pray regularly and seek the help of Our Lord and Our Lady—God's love will assist us even in times of great crisis.

The basic beliefs that we have just summarized have not changed. Whatever customs have changed, whatever Church laws have changed, the fundamental teachings of the Catholic Church remain.

The Divine and the Human

Why do we have both unchanging doctrine and changeable customs within our Church? The answer lies in the fact that in the Church we find both the grace of God and the free will of men. Our Church is made up of the divine and the human.

There was no reason, of course, that God was required to do things this way. Nevertheless, He chose to use men as His agents in bringing His Grace to us. He could have come to each of us separately in such a way that we had no dependence on others in receiving God's Revelation. Instead, God chose to come to us within a community. That means we find God's Love working through men.

It is a very difficult thing to remember both the divine and the human within the Church. There is a temptation to overlook one or the other. Perhaps in the past we sometimes forgot that there was a human element in the Church. We did not forget the divine. In fact, a strong reverence for the divine was one of the great strengths possessed by the Church of the immediate past. Nevertheless, forgetting about the human could sometimes create the impression that nothing in the Church could change. Often this was not said, but the fact was that nothing did seem to change, even with respect to customs, for a long period. This could easily create the impression that nothing would change.

If the past age tended to overlook the human element within the Church (and thus could easily come to the belief that nothing could change), the present age has exactly the opposite problem. Today many Catholics seem to overlook the divine and see only the human. This leads to the impression that practically everything in the Church can be altered, that one can explain the teachings of the Church solely by looking at human factors, as if God's Guidance played no part. This attitude in turn leads to the contempt for authority that is such a serious problem in today's Church.

The divine and the human: Let us consider each of these in turn.

The Divine

Our Catholic faith is based upon the belief that Our Lord Jesus Christ continues to guide His Church. He will safeguard His Church through all the difficulties and controversies with which the Church may be involved. This guarantee is from Jesus Himself, from the words He spoke to the Apostles after His Resurrection:

> All authority in heaven and on earth has been given to me. Go, therefore, make disciples of all the nations; baptize them in the name of the Father and of the Son and of the Holy Spirit, and teach them to observe all the commands I gave you. And know that I am with you always; yes, to the end of time. (*Matthew 28:18-20*)

The Apostles are given full authority to carry on the work of Our Lord. They are to teach and baptize all nations. They are to pass on what Christ has revealed to them. It is not their own teaching, it is not something the apostles themselves will invent: "Teach them to observe all the commands I gave you."

The authority of the Church to teach and to baptize is to remain with the Church until the end of the world. As the Apostles and their successors exercise this authority, Christ promised that He will always be with them: "And know that I am with you always; yes, to the end of time."

Out of all the Apostles, Our Lord gave a special mission and a special authority to a man named Simon. To emphasize the importance of what He was doing, Jesus gave to Simon a new proper name—the name of "Peter" which means rock. After Peter had proclaimed his faith in Jesus ("You are the Christ, the Son of the living God"), Our Lord said to Peter:

> Blessed are you, Simon son of Jona; it is not flesh and blood, it is
> my Father in heaven that has revealed this to you. And I tell you this
> in my turn, that you are Peter, and it is upon this rock that I will build
> my church; and the gates of hell shall not prevail against it; and I will
> give to you the keys of the kingdom of heaven; and whatever you shall
> bind on earth shall be bound in heaven, and whatever you shall loose
> on earth shall be loosed in heaven. (Matthew 16:16-20)

The Human

Even after they were chosen by Our Lord to be His disciples, the Apostles
were capable of failure on the human level. We see this clearly in the Gospels.
Our Lord Himself had trained them for three years. Yet, of all the Apostles,
only John remained with Our Lord under the Cross:

Prior to His Passion, Our Lord spoke these words to Peter:

> "Simon, Simon! Satan, you must know has got his wish to sift you
> all like wheat; but I have prayed for you, Simon, that your faith may
> not fail, and once you have recovered, you in turn must strengthen
> your brothers."
> "Lord," he answered, "I would be ready to go to prison with you,
> and to death."
> Jesus replied, "I tell you, Peter, by the time the cock crows today
> you will have denied three times that you know me." (*Luke
> 22:31-34 JB*)

Notice that even while predicting Peter's personal failure Jesus re-emphasizes
that He has given Peter a special role with respect to the rest of His followers.
There is a divine promise and a divine guarantee, but the person to whom
the promise is made must still struggle and can even exhibit human
shortcomings.

God's grace does not mean that things will be easy. Nor does the presence
of God's grace mean that human effort is no longer necessary. The person
who is inspired by God may have to work just as laboriously as the person
who is not. For instance, St. Luke's Gospel was inspired by the Holy Spirit.
Does this imply that the writing of the Gospel came easily for Luke? Here
are Luke's own words from the Prologue to his Gospel:

> Seeing that many others have undertaken to draw up accounts of the
> events that have taken place among us, exactly as these were handed
> down to us by those who from the outset were eyewitnesses and

ministers of the word, I in my turn, after carefully going over the whole
story from the beginning, have decided to write an ordered account
for you, Theophilus, so that your Excellency may learn how well founded the teaching is that you have received. (*Luke 1:1-4 JB*)

Although the Gospel was inspired, Luke had to do all the work that is
normal to authors. Like other writers, he had to undertake extensive research.
(Luke was not one of the original twelve Apostles). With the research completed, Luke had to consider the best way to "write an ordered account."
God's grace was not a substitute for human effort.

Because God has chosen freely to depend on men, what we do (or fail
to do) can be of great importance in God's plan. While it is true that God
will never allow His Church to be destroyed, it is also true that the failure
of Christians to cooperate with the grace of God can seriously hurt Christ's
Church, just as Our Lord Himself was seriously hurt during His lifetime
on earth by those who opposed Him. Our human response is vital.

Sometimes those Catholics who believe in the Church's divine guidance
may fail to recognize the importance of their own human activity. In today's Church, for example, those who are trying to destroy the Pope's
authority are very active. Sadly, they are applying all their talents to the
goal of undermining Church doctrine. On the other hand, those who strongly
support the Pope often stand by and do nothing. Why this relative inactivi-
ty? One reason may be the mistaken belief that they are powerless. However,
there appears to be a second reason as well, the feeling that, since God has
promised to guide His Church, any action on their part is unnecessary. On
the contrary, since God's grace comes through men, activity in support of
the Pope is indispensable. As long as those attacking the Church's teaching
authority outnumber and outwork those who actively defend that authority,
the Church will be in serious trouble.

From the very beginning, the Church has been helped by those who actively supported Her and hurt by those who attacked Her. In fact, there have
been a number of times in the Church's history when—because of the human
element—the Church has appeared to face imminent destruction. Yet, as
He promised, Christ has never abandoned His Church. Even at the darkest
moments of Her history, Our Lord has always raised up Catholics to defend the Faith. Through God's Grace, you can be one of those Catholics
today, if you accept this responsibility and work as best you can to support
the Pope.

Doctrine and Discipline

When we realize that the Church involves both the divine and the human, we can understand better why some elements in the Church can change and others cannot. It is what comes from Christ, the divine teaching, that cannot change.

Sometimes the phrase "doctrine regarding faith or morals" is used to refer to the Church's teaching. A "doctrine" is any truth taught by the Church as necessary for acceptance by the faithful. The phrase "faith and morals" means that the teaching can involve either a truth to be believed (e.g. that Our Blessed Lord is really present in the Eucharist) or a judgment about the rightness or wrongness of an action (e.g. that murder or adultery are seriously wrong). To put it another way, there is both divine teaching and divine law. The Real Presence of our Lord is a divine teaching. Murder and adultery are seriously wrong because they violate the divine law.

With respect to divine teachings and divine laws, the Church has the responsibility to proclaim them faithfully. Because they come from Christ, the Church has no power to reverse either a divine teaching or a divine law. For example, the Church cannot issue a statement announcing that adultery is no longer wrong. The Sixth Commandment—"Thou Shalt Not Commit Adultery"—is a law of God and not a regulation of the Church.

In addition to the divine, however, there are Church laws and Church customs. Our Lord told Peter: "Whatever you shall bind on earth shall be bound in heaven, and whatever you shall loose on earth shall be loosed in heaven." This does not mean that Peter has any power to change divine teaching or divine law. With respect to the divine, Peter was instructed by Jesus to "teach them to observe all the commands I gave you." Nevertheless, as the person to whom Our Lord gave "the keys of the kingdom of heaven", Peter and each of his successors have full authority from Jesus to govern His Church on earth. That includes the power to enact rules and regulations that they believe will be helpful to the Catholics of their time in carrying out the mission of Our Lord. However, they can also change these regulations—if they believe that other rules would be more appropriate. With respect to Church laws, Peter and his succesors can "bind" and "loose."

To understand why Church laws may be changed, let us consider the reasons a mother and father change the laws they make for their family. When their children are five years old, the parents have one set of regulations for them. When the children are ten, the regulations are very different. When the children are fifteen, the regulations have changed again. At all times, the goal is the same: to help their children. But what was appropriate at five may not be appropriate at ten—and what was appropriate at ten may not be appropriate at fifteen. In the same way, a Church law that was helpful at one period of time may not be helpful at another.

As the word "doctrine" is used to refer to the Church's teaching, so the word "discipline" is sometimes used to refer to those laws and regulations that are made by the Church Herself. In popular language, we often associate the word "discipline" with the word "punishment", and that is indeed one meaning of the word. In its prime meaning, however, the word "discipline" refers to the training that a person undergoes in order to achieve a certain goal.

For instance, if we turn to the sports section of our daily newspaper, we may encounter the phrase "a disciplined athlete." What does that mean? It means an individual who has trained himself through practice with respect to his ability in a sport. A disciplined athlete differs from an undisciplined athlete who may have much natural talent in the sport but who had not worked to bring this talent to its most perfect state. Similarly, we can speak of a "disciplined writer" or a "disciplined speaker." In the same way, discipline within the Church refers to everything that the Church Herself devises in order to help us lead the Christian life.

In the previous examples, we considered "disciplined" individuals. The Church, of course, is not simply one person. The Church is all of us united in Christ. Therefore, it might help to look at discipline as it exists within a group.

Instead of a single disciplined athlete, suppose that we have a group of athletes. If they want to form a team, they must develop a group discipline in addition to their personal discipline. They must coordinate their individual talents in order to function effectively. On a football team, some people will carry the ball while others will block. The coach of the football team has the responsibility to train the group so that the "team discipline" is as effective as possible.

Because a coordinated group effort is involved, the effectiveness of the group can be damaged severly if individuals decide on their own to ignore or abandon the group discipline. If a football player who is supposed to block says to himself, "I want some variety, so instead of blocking, I think that I will run downfield," then the entire team is hurt.

Does this mean that an individual player cannot suggest to the coach an effective play or recommend a change in the team's strategy that he thinks will be helpful? Not at all. What it does mean, however, is that he cannot put his desired change into effect by himself. For the effectiveness of the group, he must follow the current "team discipline," even if he hopes that in the future he will be able to persuade the coach to make the change.

Change Within the Church

Now let us apply what has been said about "discipline" to the Church.

What are some of the Church's regulations that could be changed?

If we consider the Mass, for example, we find some elements that cannot be altered but others that could change. The meaning and the basic action of the Mass must always remain the same because they come from Christ. The bread and wine consecrated by an ordained priest become the Body and Blood of Our Lord as the priest repeats the words of Our Lord at the Last Supper. This can never be modified. Nevertheless, the Church can—as She has through the centuries—add or remove prayers from the Mass. The Church can change the language in which the Mass is said, as American Catholics experienced in the 1960's when English replaced Latin as the language of the Mass. Such elements are not essential to the meaning of the Mass, and the Church makes these changes based upon the belief that they will help us to participate better in the Mass.

In the 1960's, the Church also changed her discipline with respect to Friday abstinence from meat. The purpose of the Friday abstinence regulation was to have us all do the same thing on a particular day, to offer a group sacrifice on the day that Our Lord died. Now, with the exception of the Fridays of Lent, this requirement no longer exists. Why? Because the judgment was reached that it might be better if each Catholic chose a personal sacrifice instead of having the same penance for everyone.

Now suppose that a Church disciplinary law has been changed. Would it be wrong to prefer the previous situation to the present one? No, it would not. What is involved here is discipline and not doctrine. In a later chapter, we will be considering both the infallibility of the Pope and the necessity of Catholics to give religious assent to the teaching of the Holy Father on faith and morals. However, as the phrase "faith and morals" indicates, both infallibility and religious assent pertain to doctrine. With one exception (which we will discuss in a following chapter), they do not apply to disciplinary matters.

Why? Because a change in Church discipline does not involve a change in the teachings of Christ but a practical judgment about the present situation. When a change in Church discipline is being discussed, the question before the Church is: "What Church regulations will be of most help to Catholics in living the Christian life?"

Since the Church does not claim to be infallible with respect to such a practical decision, one may feel in his heart that it would have been better if a particular change (such as the change in Friday abstinence) had not been made. Or—looking to the future—one may believe that the Church ought to change its present discipline (not its doctrine) in some respect.

But can we go further? Is it permisssible to voice a private feeling publicly? Can we work with others in the Church to bring about the disciplinary change that we consider desirable?

In general, the answer is "yes"—provided we work in the right way. I say "in general" because the Pope, as Vicar of Christ, does have the authority to decide that public discussion about a disciplinary matter should cease, if the Holy Father believes that such public discussion is harmful to the Church. In practice, however, such a request is rarely made. In the absence of such a statement by the Pope, it is quite permissible for us to work for those changes in the Church's discipline that we consider desirable.

But we must do it in the right way. That means two things. First, even while working for a particular change, we must continue to respect and follow the discipline that presently exists. Second, we must express ourselves in a way that does not attack the authority of the Pope or undermine his ability to lead the Church. It is one thing to tell the Pope how a particular change has affected us and to give our views about possible changes in the future. It is quite another thing to launch a public-relations campaign designed to pressure the Pope into doing what we want.

If we have the right attitude, then it is not only permissible but even desirable and important for us to tell Church authorities how changes in discipline are affecting our spiritual life. Remember that the purpose of the Church's discipline is to help us to be better Catholics. Therefore, the Church can benefit from our "feed-back." How can Church authorities know whether or not a change has helped us unless we tell them about our experience and our attitudes? Furthermore, if we are silent, and if another group of people are not silent but communicate their views to Church authorities, and if this group has a different attitude than we do with respect to a change in the Church discipline, then we should not be surprised if Church authorities soon become more sensitive to the attitudes of this other group than to our own attitudes.

Three examples may illustrate the legitimacy and importance of telling Church authorities how developments in the Church are affecting us. The first example is the 1981 letter of the Apostolic Delegate that we have quoted previously. Note that the Vatican was concerned precisely because a number of Catholics had written to the Pope to tell him that their faith was being undermined by the attacks on Church doctrine that were appearing in Catholic newspapers. Far from resenting such unsolicited letters or dismissing them as out of place, Rome welcomed the information and urged the bishops of the United States to correct the problem.

How many people wrote to the Pope? We do not know, but I would imagine that for every Catholic who wrote there were at least a thousand Catholics who felt the same way but who did not think it appropriate to write. (A major purpose of this book is to encourage all of these people to speak up in the future. If this happens, the defenders of Catholic doctrine will be strengthened greatly.)

A short time before the Apostolic Delegate's letter, the Vatican wrote another letter to the American bishops. This letter requested information about the attitudes of American Catholics with respect to the Latin Mass. Was there a desire on the part of many Catholics in America for a Latin Mass and would such a Mass fulfill a spiritual need for Catholics? Again we see a desire on the part of Rome to know about the effect of a disciplinary change on the spiritual life of Catholics.

Perhaps the most dramatic American example of Church authorities seeking to know public opinion about a disciplinary change occurred in 1969. The bishops of the United States were considering possible changes in discipline with respect to the six holydays of obligation. Should the requirement of attending Mass on the six holydays be eliminated? Or should the requirement be kept for some of the holydays but eliminated for the others? Or should the present discipline be retained in its entirety?

A decision was made to poll the Catholic laity. A number of cities were selected at random, and the Catholic people in these areas were given an opportunity to vote on the question. The result? A strong vote from the laity for keeping the traditional discipline on all six holydays.

These three examples show clearly both the importance of expressing our views and the desire of the Pope to know how disciplinary change is affecting us.

One reason the Church desires to know our reaction is that She realizes that disciplinary change can have unexpected effects on people. Sometimes a change can be made for the best of reasons. Logically, it can seem to be the only thing to do. Yet the change has a serious psychological effect on the very people it was supposed to help.

I know of an elderly couple who recently left the home where they had lived for 52 years—their entire married life. At the urging of their two sons, they moved forty miles away to the country town where both of their children now lived. Their sons had excellent reasons for encouraging this change. First, their parents were nearly eighty and lived by themselves. Second, a high crime rate had developed in the section of the city where the parents were living and the two sons were worried that their mother and father might not be safe.

On the logical level, the move was all for the best. Nevertheless, after the change was made, the children soon noticed that their parents were most unhappy. The entire life of the mother and father had been spent in a particular neighborhood. Suddenly that neighborhood had been removed from them. How could they simply discard the customs and traditions of a lifetime?

In considering the desirability of change, the sons had looked at the old neighborhood from a logical viewpoint. For the parents, however, it was not a matter of logic but of their very psychological identity. Who they were was intimately tied up with the neighborhood where they had spent a lifetime.

Should the parents have stayed where they were? Perhaps. Yet perhaps not, for there were excellent reasons for the change. What can be said is this. If their sons had foreseen the psychological effect that the change could have, possibly the good effects of the move could have been achieved without breaking all ties with the old neighborhood.

In the same way, the disciplinary changes in the Church have been made for excellent logical reasons. Nevertheless, it appears clear that these changes have also had a severe and largely unforseen psychological effect upon many Catholics who feel as if they were suddenly and unexpectedly removed from the "religious neighborhood" in which they had lived all their lives.

Not everyone, of course, has been affected in this way. Many Catholics either welcomed the changes or at least had no difficulty in accepting them. But those for whom this is not the case should write to the Pope and the Bishops and tell them about the affect that the change has had on them. If they know other Catholics who have had a similar reaction, then they should write also.

Thus, if Church authority hears that an unexpected adverse effect has been produced on many Catholics by a disciplinary change, this will increase the likelihood of finding a way to keep the good results of the change while at the same time helping with very real spiritual problems connected with it. Therefore, no one should ever feel embarrassed or hesitant to write the Church authorities about the effect that a change in Church discipline has had on his spiritual life. At the same time, however, we must remember that such questions do not involve the heart of the Catholic faith. No change in Church discipline has taken away what comes from Christ, and no change ever will. If we are to lose some of the old and valued Church customs, then perhaps this is the sacrifice that Christ wants us to make. We certainly have every right to work not to lose these customs. But, if it is not to be, then this very act of sacrifice can be a way of saying to Our Lord, "I love You".

3.
The Authority of the Pope

In the last chapter, we concentrated upon the feeling of loss that many Catholics experience because of a change in Church customs that they have cherished. We were thinking primarily of situations in which the previous Church discipline has been modified by the Pope and the bishops.

In many other circumstances, however, the change has not been made by the Pope but by somebody else. The alteration involved may even be against the known wishes of the Holy Father. Nevertheless, somebody on the local level decides to make the change. As a result, the Catholic people are deprived of cherished devotional practices that the Pope wants them to have.

In my experience, when Catholics who loved the customs of the past talk about their confusion and sense of loss in today's Church, they are usually referring to unauthorized changes rather than to legitimate modifications of Church discipline.

Recently a Catholic newspaper carried an interview with a priest who explained the "problems" he faced in his parish. According to the priest, a major "problem" was that many of his parishioners had what the priest referred to as a "pre-Vatican II" mentality. The priest spoke of the Rosary as an example, for some of his "pre-Vatican II" parishioners had requested him to stress the Rosary as an important parish devotion. Without denying them the right to say the Rosary themselves (what remarkable tolerance on his part!), the priest refused the request of his parishioners. He explained to them that devotional practices in the Church had undergone many changes since the Second Vatican Council.

Here is some news for this priest: The Holy Father agrees with his "pre-Vatican II" parishioners and not with him. Every Pope since Vatican II has cherished the Rosary as much as his predecessors. For example, in 1974 Pope Paul VI urged all Catholic families to pray the Rosary. In the Pope's own words:

> We now desire, as a continuation of the thought of our predecessors, to recommend strongly the recitation of the family rosary . . . There is no doubt that . . . the rosary should be considered as one of the best and most efficacious prayers in common that the Christian family is invited to recite. We like to think and sincerely hope that when the family gathering becomes a time of prayer the rosary is a frequent and favorite manner of praying.

In 1981, in his Apostolic Exhortation on the Family, Pope John Paul II repeated the call of Paul VI. After quoting his predecessor, Pope John Paul added his own comments about the great value of the rosary. "In this way," wrote John Paul II,

> authentic devotion to Mary, which finds expression in sincere love and generous imitation of the Blessed Virgin's interior spiritual attitude, constitutes a special instrument for nourishing loving communion in the family and for developing conjugal and family spirituality. For she who is the mother of Christ and of the Church is in a special way the mother of Christian families, of domestic churches.

Nevertheless, despite the desires of the Popes, many parishes no longer stress the Rosary as they once did. Why? Because somebody on the parish level preferring his own attitude on the Rosary to the view of the Pope, has not hesitated to use his local power in such a manner as to turn the parish away from its previous devotional practice.

The example of the "modern" pastor and his "pre-Vatican II" parishioners illustrates an interesting tactic often employed by those who reject the views of the Holy Father. They claim that the Second Vatican Council somehow justifies their actions and they try to create the impression that Catholics who support the Pope have been "outdated" by the Council.

Even Mother Teresa of Calcutta was treated in this manner when she visited the United States in 1981. Recognizing her truly remarkable work among the poor of India and twenty other countries, the world-at-large greeted Mother Teresa with interest and respect. Unfortunately, there was an important exception. Certain Catholics were offended by Mother Teresa's "pre-Vatican II" attitudes. Especially outspoken in this regard were some Catholic sisters who considered themselves to be leaders of the "feminist movement" within the Catholic Church. To understand the reason that Mother Teresa disturbed them, it might be helpful to look at what these women religious were doing at the time of Mother Teresa's arrival in the United States.

As reported in the *New York Times*, the "feminist" American sisters had found a unique way to express their rebellion against Church authority. They were holding their own "Masses" without the presence of an ordained priest. The *Times* correctly noted that in the official view of the Church such "Masses" were not only invalid but regarded as blasphemous and as a great scandal. Nevertheless, the women religious vowed to continue. "It is necessary for us to recast all our symbols and traditions," was the way one sister put it to the *Times*. The sister went on to add that her group had even discussed whether to replace the bread and wine with something more "appropriate" for a "women's liturgy."

In the middle of all this, Mother Teresa arrives. Why had she come to our country? Out of respect for the Holy Father. Pope John Paul II had requested her to make such a journey and Mother Teresa immediately put aside her own plans when she heard of the Pope's desires. And why had the Pope asked her to come? A major reason was to support the Church's teaching on birth control, the very teaching that many of the feminist sisters had mocked openly for years.

Instead of proclaiming "sisterhood is powerful" and shaking her fist at the Vatican, the woman religious from India made it known that her whole life was based on her reverence for Church authority. Instead of advocating the distribution of contraceptives to the poor, Mother Teresa said bluntly that contraception and abortion had brought a great spiritual poverty to the world.

Such a person had to be "pre-Vatican II". Whatever her work in India, the feminist sisters "knew" that the convictions expressed by Mother Teresa could not possibly be meaningful to today's world, although the stupid world seemed not to understand this fact since the world had awarded Mother Teresa the Nobel Prize. It should be added quickly, of course, that many, many American sisters agree with Mother Teresa and not with the feminist sisters. As with other Catholics who support the Holy Father, these women religious have strong convictions but they often do not organize themselves into groups in order to work actively for their beliefs. This allows the feminist sisters to create the false impression that they represent the women religious of America. It also allows the feminist sisters to gain increasing influence, since an organized minority—no matter how radical—is usually far more effective than an unorganized majority.

As can be observed from the activities of the feminist sisters, it is not only the Church's discipline but the Church's unchanging doctrine that is under attack. This attack extends even to the most basic Catholic beliefs: the divinity of Our Lord, His Resurrection from the dead, the Real Presence of Jesus in the Holy Eucharist. Since these central Catholic doctrines are vigorously defended by the Holy Father, a major goal of the dissenters is to persuade as many Catholics as possible to ignore or reject the authority of the Pope. Therefore, let us consider the question of authority, and, since those challenging the Holy Father falsely suggest that their position has been justified by the Vatican Council, let us begin by quoting what the Council has actually said on this subject.

The Vatican Council on the Authority of the Pope

This sacred synod, following in the steps of the First Vatican Council, teaches and declares with it that Jesus Christ, the eternal pastor, set up the holy Church by entrusting the apostles with their mission, as He Himself had been sent by the Father (cf. Jn. 20-21). He willed that their successors, the bishops namely, should be the shepherds in his Church until the end of the world. In order that the episcopate itself, however, might be one and undivided he put Peter at the head of the other apostles, and in him he set up a lasting and visible source and foundation of the unity both of faith and of communion. This teaching concerning the institution, the permanence, the nature and import of the sacred primacy of the Roman Pontiff and his infallible teaching office, the sacred synod proposes anew to be firmly believed by all the faithful, and, proceeding undeviatingly with this same undertaking, it proposes to proclaim publicly and enunciate clearly the doctrine concerning bishops, successors of the apostles, who together with Peter's successor, the Vicar of Christ and the visible head of the whole Church, direct the house of the living God.

The Lord Jesus, having prayed at length to the Father, called to himself those whom he willed and appointed twelve to be with him, whom he might send to preach the kingdom of God (cf. Mk 3:13-19; Mt. 10:1-42). These apostles (cf. Lk. 6:13) he constituted in the form of a college or permanent assembly, at the head of which he placed Peter, chosen from amongst them (cf. Jn. 21:15-1 7). He sent them first of all to the children of Israel and then to all peoples (cf. Rom. 1:16), so that, sharing in his power, they might make all peoples his disciples and sanctify and govern them (cf. Mt. 28:16-20; Mk. 16:15; Lk. 24:45-48; Jn. 20:21-23) and thus spread the Church and, administering it under the guidance of the Lord, shepherd it all days until the end of the world (cf. Mt. 28:20). They were fully confirmed in this mission on the day of Pentecost (cf. Acts 2:1-26) according to the promise of the Lord: "You shall receive power when the Holy Ghost descends upon you; and you shall be my witnesses both in

Jerusalem and in all Judea and Samaria, and to the remotest part of the earth'' (Acts 1:8). By preaching everywhere the Gospel (cf. Mk. 16:20), welcomed and received under the influence of the Holy Spirit by those who hear it, the apostles gather together the universal Church, which the Lord founded upon the apostles and built upon blessed Peter their leader, the chief cornerstone being Christ Jesus himself (cf. Apoc. 21:14; Mt. 16:18, Eph. 2:20).

That divine mission, which was committed by Christ to the Apostles, is destined to last until the end of the world (cf. Mt. 28:20), since the Gospel, which they were charged to hand on, is, for the Church, the principle of all its life for all time. For that very reason the apostles were careful to appoint successors in this hierarchically constituted society . . .

The college or body of bishops has for all that no authority unless united with the Roman Pontiff, Peter's successor, as its head, whose primatial authority, let it be added, over all, whether pastors or faithful, remains in its integrity. For the Roman Pontiff, by reason of his office as Vicar of Christ, namely, and as pastor of the entire Church, has full, supreme and universal power over the whole Church, a power which he can always exercise unhindered. The order of bishops is the successor to the college of the apostles in their role as teachers and pastors, and in it the apostolic college is perpetuated. Together with their head, the Supreme Pontiff, and never apart from him, they have supreme and full authority over the universal Church; but this power cannot be exercised without the agreement of the Roman Pontiff. The Lord made Peter alone the rock-foundation and the holder of the keys of the Church (cf. Mt. 16:18-19), and constituted him shepherd of his whole flock (cf. Jn. 21:15ff). It is clear, however, that the office of binding and loosing which was given to Peter (Mt. 16:19), was also assigned to the college of the apostles united to its head (Mt. 18:18; 28:16-20). This college, in so far as it is composed of many members, is the expression of the multifariousness and universality of the People of God and of the unity of the flock of Christ, in so far as it is assembled under one head. In it the bishops, while loyally respecting the primacy and pre-eminence of their head, exercise their own proper authority for the good of their faithful, indeed even for the good of the whole Church, the organic structure and harmony of which are strengthened by the continued influence of the Holy Spirit. The supreme authority over the whole Church, which this college possesses, is exercised in a solemn way in an ecumenical council. There never is an ecumenical council which is not confirmed or at least recognized as such by Peter's successor. And it is the prerogative of the Roman Pontiff to convoke such councils, to preside over them and to confirm them. This same collegiate power can be exercised in union with the Pope by the bishops while living in different parts of the world, provided

the head of the college summon them to collegiate action, or at least approve or freely admit the corporate action of the unassembled bishops, so that a truly collegiate act may result.
(Dogmatic Constitution on the Church, *Lumen Gentium*, Chapter 3, Nos. 18, 19, 20, 22, 23)

Notice how clear the Vatican Council is with regard to the authority of the Holy Father. Even when developing the very important truth that the bishops are the successors of the apostles, the Council goes out of its way to stress the primacy of the Pope. United with the Holy Father, a council of the bishops that is general and universal ("ecumenical") has full authority to act for the Church. Separated from the Holy Father, such a council has no authority at all, even if every other bishop in the world were to participate: "This power cannot be exercised without the agreement of the Roman Pontiff."

Is it simply a current Church law that the decisions of an ecumenical council have no authority unless they are approved by the Pope? No. As Vatican II teaches, what is involved here is something that comes from Our Lord, namely, the authority that Jesus gave to Peter and his successors. The Vatican Council re-affirms as Biblical teaching the truth that Peter alone is the rock on which Jesus has built His Church. Peter alone has been given the keys of the Church. Peter alone has been made shepherd of the whole flock. As legitimate Apostles, the others share with Peter the power to "bind and loose," but only if they are united with Peter in their actions.

Because of the special mission that Jesus gave to Peter, the Vatican Council concludes that "there never is an ecumenical council which is not confirmed or at least recognized as such by Peter's successor." Furthermore, Vatican II expressly teaches that, while the decisions of a general council require the subsequent approval by the Pope in order to be valid, the decisions of the Pope do *not* require the subsequent approval by a general council in order to be valid. In the words that perhaps best sum up the teaching of the Church with regard to the authority of the Holy Father, Vatican II tells us: "For the Roman Pontiff, by reason of his office as Vicar of Christ, namely, and as pastor of the entire Church, has full, supreme and universal power over the whole Church, a power which he can always exercise unhindered."

"Why Him and Not Me?"

Those Catholics who attack the authority of the Pope have the attitude: "Why him and not us? Why should the Pope have such authority?" For one reason only. Jesus Christ freely chose to do things this way.

There is something seriously wrong with the outlook of people who call themselves Catholic but whose only reaction to the authority of the Pope is one of irritation. Instead of praising the Lord for the wonderful gift He has given to us, they can only complain that Jesus did not construct His Church in the way they would want.

To appreciate fully what is involved in such an attitude, let us suppose that instead of being born two thousand years ago Our Lord had chosen to be born today. He is born in a town only five miles away from us. Like the shepherds at Bethlehem, we are one of the first to hear the news. We run next door and joyfully tell our neighbor: "The Lord has come. He has been born in the next town!"

Instead of reacting with gladness, however, our neighbor proceeds to throw a temper tantrum. "How dare the Lord choose the next town! Our town is as good. I'm highly insulted that we are expected to go five miles to the next town in order to see Christ!"

Our neighbor is obsessed with what is basically a matter of pride, the prestige of his town as compared with the prestige of the next town. His town must be first. Instead of appreciating the good news that Christ has come, he resents the fact that the next town has been honored.

In the same way, those Catholics who resent the authority of the Holy Father are obsessed with what is basically a matter of pride, their prestige as compared with the prestige of the Pope. They must be first. Instead of appreciating the good news that Our Lord has founded His Church, they are angry that Our Lord asks them to accept the authority of the Holy Father.

It was the free choice of Jesus to be born in Bethlehem instead of in Rome or Athens. Should the Romans and the Greeks have felt insulted? It was the free choice of Jesus to live in the first century instead of in the 15th or the 20th centuries. Should the people of these later times feel insulted? It was the free choice of Jesus to choose Peter and his successors and to give the Popes full authority to act in His Name. Should Catholics who are not the Pope feel insulted? Not if they understand what the Lord has done for us.

To use an example employed by Jesus Himself, we have been invited to the Lord's own banquet. Instead of fighting for the first seats at the table, we should thank God for the wonderful gift He has given to us.

The Office and the Person of the Papacy

In studying the authority of the Pope, the key is to understand that the Papacy is an office. In addition to its internal life, every society—because it is also something external—needs a structure consisting of offices. An office carries with it both responsibilities and privileges. In our United States, we have offices such as President, Senator, Supreme Court Justice. Within the Church, Our Lord established the office of the Papacy and the office of the Episcopacy; and He gave to the Pope and the bishops the necessary authority to carry out their mission.

It is important to distinguish the office from the holiness or other qualities of the person who occupies the office. In our American society, the President of the United States occupies the highest office. That in itself does not necessarily make him the best citizen. Americans who hold no office at all may be just as patriotic as the person who holds the highest office.

The same is true of the Pope. Holiness, our closeness to Christ, our union of love with Him, depends on the person, not on the office. We wrote previously about Mother Teresa of Calcutta. It could well be that such a saintly figure is holier than 99 percent of the bishops. Nevertheless, Mother Teresa reverences and follows the bishops and the Pope. Why? Because of her respect for the office that they hold and her recognition that Christ has founded this office.

We can appreciate this distinction even more clearly if we look at the apostles themselves. It was Peter, not John, who was chosen by Jesus to be the first Pope, despite the fact that John appears to have been personally superior to Peter in many respects.

Can one imagine, for example, the case that John could have made against Peter, if like some Catholics today, he wanted to reject Peter's authority. He could have said to Peter: "I was the one, not you, who remained faithful to the Lord and did not desert Him at the Crucifixion. I was the one, not you, to whom Jesus entrusted His Mother."

As we learn about the Apostles from the New Testament, John appears to be far more intelligent than Peter. He was also closer personally to the Lord. Despite all these qualities, John willingly accepted the authority of Peter. Again, why? Because Our Lord chose Peter and not John to occupy the office of the first Pope. Jesus chose John to do many other wonderful things but He did not select John to be the Pope. The office, therefore, is not something that comes because of one's superior personal qualities but one that Our Lord freely gives to whomever He will.

That the most talented Apostle did not hold the highest office was something that required humility from both John and Peter. The one had to obey a person who was less capable than himself, while the other had to exercise the authority given to him despite the personal knowledge that some of the people he was leading were superior to him in many ways.

Nevertheless, both Peter and John trusted in the Lord.

Peter's humility can be seen even in the Gospel accounts of his failures. If we think about it, most of these accounts must have come from Peter himself. For example, among the early followers of Christ, who but Peter was present at the moment he denied Our Lord three times? Rarely has any leader been as open as Peter in admitting his personal shortcomings. Perhaps St. Peter's purpose in giving such publicity and such emphasis to his individual mistakes was to make certain that all Christians understood that he was to be followed because of the office given to him by Jesus and not because of any personal brilliance.

John's humility and respect for Peter's authority can be seen in the Gospel account of the Resurrection. Both Apostles are told by Mary Magdalen that the stone has been removed from Our Lord's tomb. John can run faster than Peter and he arrives at the tomb first. Instead of proceeding further, however, he restrains his eagerness and waits for Peter to catch up with him. Then John steps aside so that Peter can be the first to enter the tomb.

The message involved in the relationship between John and Peter is one that has great relevance for the present. Those Catholics who attack the authority of the Pope base their challenge upon the belief that they are more intelligent or capable than the Holy Father.

In passing, it might be added that this claim is highly questionable. While the critics of the Pope apparently consider their own genius to be dazzlingly obvious, such brilliance is not at all apparent to the rest of us. Nevertheless, let us suppose for a moment that their self-evaluation is correct and that the dissenters are veritable supermen—the most superb examples of talent and intelligence ever to walk the face of the earth.

So what? The authority of the Pope is not something that depends on personal qualities. The authority of the Pope comes from the office given him by Christ Himself. Ability and genius—whether real or imagined—does not excuse us from the responsibility of following humbly the teaching of the Lord, including the teaching of the Lord on the role of Peter in His Church.

Authority of Expertise and of Office

The reason it is essential to emphasize that the authority of the Holy Father comes from the office that he occupies, and not from his personal qualities, is that there are two kinds of "authority".

Sometimes the word "authority" is used as a synonym for the word "expert." For example, we speak of an authority on the game of bridge. This means a bridge expert. Or we speak of an authority on history. This refers to a person who is very learned in that field.

However, the word "authority" can also be used in a way that is not equivalent to the word "expert". When used in this other sense, the word "authority" refers to the "decision-making power" that is possessed by a person who occupies an office within a society. If his office gives him the power to act in a certain area, then the office-holder has the "authority" to make binding decisions.

This distinction between the two meanings of "authority" is crucial because it directly affects our responsibility to obey authority. When "authority" does *not* refer to an office, we are free to accept or reject it. In other words, the choice is up to us whether to agree with the opinion of an "expert." On the one hand, we probably ought to give some weight to the expert's advice because of his special knowledge. On the other hand, the "weight" that we give is not necessarily decisive. We may value our own expertise in the matter under discussion . . . or we may know of other "experts" who disagree with the views of the "expert" to whom we are speaking . . . or we may simply see no valid reason to follow the "expert's" opinion.

In summary, the proper attitude toward "authority" in the sense of "expert" could be expressed as follows: "I will listen closely to what you say . . . but, if I am not convinced by your reasoning, then I may act otherwise."

With respect to "authority" in the sense of "office", there is a very different operating principle from that which exists for the "expert." It is not just a matter of giving "weight" to the office-holder's views. Rather, if the office-holder is exercising the legitimate authority of his office, we can be bound to follow his decision. Our responsibility to obey is not lessened by the fact that we may disagree with the reasoning of the office-holder. Our personal approval or disapproval is irrelevant.

To illustrate what is involved, let us suppose that you are driving your car on a Sunday afternoon. Sitting next to you in the front seat is a friend of yours who happens to be an expert auto-mechanic. After five or ten miles, he says to you: "I think you ought to pull over to the side of the road and check out your car." You respond: "For what reason? I don't notice any problem with the driving of this car. I'll certainly listen to whatever arguments you present, and, if you can convince me there is something wrong, then I will pull over to the side of the road. Until I am convinced on the merits of the case, however, I'm not going to stop this car."

This is your right—precisely because your friend is not exercising any office which gives him the authority to order you to pull over to the side of the road. On the other hand, suppose that a few moments later you sud-

denly hear a police whistle behind you. When you stop at the next red traffic light, a policeman on a motorcycle comes up to you and says: "Pull
that car over to the side of the road."

Giving the very same speech that you just presented to your friend, you
reply: "Officer, I respectfully request you to tell me the reasons that you
are asking me to pull over. I assure you that I will listen very closely to
your arguments and if you can convince me intellectually that there is sufficient reason to pull over to the side of the road, then I am prepared to do so."

I think we all know what would happen if we expressed ourselves in
that way to a policeman. Why? Because in virtue of his office, the policeman
has the authority to regulate traffic. That includes the authority to tell us
to pull our car to the side of the road. We have the obligation to obey the
policeman's authority even if we do not understand the reasons for his direc-
tive. While the auto mechanic sitting next to us may know more about cars
than the policeman, it is the policeman who has been given the office of
regulating traffic in our civil society. Therefore, we must follow the officer's
ruling even if we ourselves do not agree with it.

Let us apply the same criteria to another situation. Suppose we are
lawyers who are arguing a case before a judge. We are specialists in the
particular area of the law on which the case turns. We honestly believe we
are far more knowledgeable than the judge on the matter in question. When
the judge makes his ruling, does our expertise give us the right to say: "Your
Honor, I can only accept your ruling if I personally am convinced it is right:
Please be assured that I will give weight to your views . . . but I must also
give weight to the views of those I consider to be experts on this subject.
If their arguments seem to be superior to yours, then I must follow them
and not you."

If any individuals responded in this manner to a judge, their fate would
be the same as with the policeman. Civil society would regard such a position as a direct attack upon the order that is necessary for the functioning
of the community, and, if the dissenters persisted in such an attitude, they
would end up in jail. Why does society react so strongly? Basically for the
reason that, both in the case of the policeman and in the case of the judge,
what the dissenters are really doing is to advocate a kind of anarchy. They
are rejecting any authority that is based upon the office a person holds, while
accepting only that "authority" that comes from personal expertise. Furthermore, they are leaving to the personal judgment of each individual the
decision about which directives of the office-holder to follow and which
to ignore. No community can survive under such a principle.

While few of us would put forth such anarchical views with respect to a policeman (an "officer of the law") or a judge (an "officer of the court"), the rejection of any teaching authority based upon office is a widespread attitude in today's Church. As one example, a noted priest-dissenter from the Pope's authority recently appeared on television to promote a novel he had written. When asked for his views about the Holy Father, the priest responded by praising the Pope for his personal qualities but criticizing the Pope for his support of the official Church teaching on faith and morals. According to the priest-dissenter, the "Catholics of today" (by which he meant the Catholics who agreed with him) were more "mature" than those Catholics of past ages who felt they had to believe all the Church's doctrines. To the contrary, he and his fellow Catholics had a "pick and choose" attitude with respect to Church teaching. They would decide for themselves what to believe and what to deny and they would pay absolutely no attention to any directives from the Holy Father that they judged "irrelevant."

It would be hard to find a better description of anarchy, the denial of all authority based upon office. Like the priest-novelist, those Catholics who deny the authority of the Pope's office frequently soften their criticism by lauding the Holy Father's "personal charisma." They suggest that such personal qualities represent the only "authority" they will accept.

St. Peter must be turning over in his grave at such an attitude, for this is precisely the view that the first Pope worked so hard against. It is certainly a wonderful thing if a Pope possesses either intellectual brilliance or the kind of inspirational personality that attracts large numbers of people. These are personal talents that can be a big help to the Holy Father in his defense of the Church's teaching. Nevertheless, the authority of the Pope does not depend on these attributes, just as the authority of a policeman does not depend upon whether he can speak with a deep-sounding voice. Whether such personal qualities are present or absent, the authority of the office remains exactly the same.

The authority of any office-holder is determined by both the scope and the origin of his office. With respect to scope, the office may be limited or unlimited. In the examples we discussed earlier, the policeman has authority over traffic but he does not have authority to decide a court case. The judge has authority in the courtroom but not on the highway.

As Vatican II teaches, the authority of the Pope with regard to Church matters is unlimited ("For the Roman Pontiff, by reason of his office as Vicar of Christ, namely, and as pastor of the entire Church, has full, supreme and universal power over the whole Church, a power which he can always exercise unhindered.") The authority of the office is unlimited because that is the way it was established by Jesus, Who gave Peter—and the other apostles united with Peter—the mission of teaching "all nations" to observe "all the commands I gave you" until "the end of time."

Because the offices of Pope and Bishops were established by Jesus Himself, the Church is different from any civil society, where the offices are usually created by the people who live in that society. Because all civil offices are man-made, it is entirely possible for even the highest civil authority to make a decision that is directly contrary to the law of God. In the United States, this happened in 1973 when the Supreme Court legalized the killing of unborn children. Since in any conflict we must always choose God's law over man's, we have no obligation whatever to obey civil authority when it commands us to violate the law of God. While such a situation is always possible on the civil level, Our Lord Himself has guaranteed His Church that this kind of conflict will never occur when the Pope exercises His solemn teaching authority. Thus, while Catholics may sometimes be justified in dissenting on religious grounds from the decision of the state, there is no such thing as a valid Catholic dissent from the religious teaching of the Holy Father.

4.
The Extraordinary Magisterium, The Ordinary Magisterium and Infallibility

When the Holy Father teaches officially on faith and morals, he can exercise his authority in one of two ways. In almost all situations, the Pope employs what is referred to as the "ordinary magisterium." On very special occasions, however, the Pope will exercise his "extraordinary magisterium."

The word "magisterium" simply means "teaching authority." "Ordinary" refers to the fact that this is the usual way of teaching, while "extraordinary" means that this is the method employed in exceptional circumstances.

Two other words are also used frequently in connection with the Holy Father's teaching office—*ex cathedra* and "authentic."

Ex cathedra is a Latin phrase that can be translated literally as "from the chair"—in other words, "officially." When the Pope speaks *ex cathedra*, he is speaking in virtue of his office as the Vicar of Christ. "Authentic" also means "official." Despite the similarity in their literal meaning, however, the phrase *ex cathedra* is often used to refer to the extraordinary magisterium, while the word "authentic" is employed with a broader meaning to include both the extraordinary magisterium and the ordinary magisterium. Thus, the "ordinary" teaching authority of the Holy Father is sometimes described as "authentic teaching that is not *ex cathedra*".

With this background, let us consider what the Church Herself has said about the "extraordinary" and "ordinary" teaching authority of the Holy Father. Here are five official statements of the Catholic Church. As a summary and a guide, the major questions addressed by each statement have been put in a parenthesis before the quotation itself.

The first two statements—Vatican I and Vatican II—consider the extraordinary magisterium of the Holy Father. The third statement, from Pope Paul VI, can be applied to both the extraordinary magisterium and to the ordinary magisterium. The fourth and fifth statements—Vatican II and Pius XII—refer to the ordinary magisterium.

Extraordinary Magisterium

[Questions covered: Is it an article of faith that the Holy Father can teach infallibly? When does the Pope exercise his "extraordinary magisterium?" Is it necessary to obtain the consent of other people within the Church before the Pope can make an infallible statement?]

It is a dogma divinely revealed: that the Roman Pontiff when he speaks *ex cathedra*, that is, when acting in the office of shepherd and teacher of all Christians, he defines, by virtue of his supreme apostolic authority, doctrine concerning faith and morals to be held by the universal Church posseses through the divine assistance promised to him in the person of St. Peter, the infallibility with which the divine Redeemer willed his Church to be endowed in defining doctrine concerning faith or morals; and that such definitions are therefore irreformable of themselves, and not from the consent of the Church.
(*The Teaching of the Catholic Church*, The Church on Earth, VIII: The Pope: Vicar of Christ, Par. 6)

[Questions covered: Does Vatican II reaffirm in all respects the teaching of Vatican I concerning the infalliblity of the Holy Father? When a doctrine regarding faith or morals is defined either by the Pope alone or by the body of bishops in union with the Pope, does Vatican II recognize a right of Catholics to dissent from that teaching? Or, on the contrary, does Vatican II teach that all Catholics are bound to adhere and obliged to assent to such a teaching?]

This teaching concerning the institution, the permanence, the nature and import of the sacred primacy of the Roman Pontiff and his infallible teaching office, the sacred synod proposed anew to be firmly believed by all the faithful . . .
(*The Dogmatic Constitution on the Church* par. 18)
This infalliblity, however, with which the divine redeemer wished to endow his Church in defining doctrine pertaining to faith and morals, is co-extensive with the deposit of revelation, which must be religiously guarded and loyally and courageously expounded. The Roman Pontiff, head of the college of bishops, enjoys this infallibility in virtue of his office, when, a supreme pastor and teacher of all the faithful— who confirms his brethren in the faith (cf. Luke 22:32)—he proclaims

in an absolute decision a doctrine pertaining to faith or morals. For that reason his definitions are rightly said to be irreformable by their very nature and not by reason of the assent of the Church, in as much as they were made with the assistance of the Holy Spirit promised to him in the person of blessed Peter himself; and as a consequence they are in no way in need of the approval of others, and do not admit of appeal to any other tribunal. For in such a case the Roman Pontiff does not utter a pronouncement as a private person, but rather does he expound and defend the teaching of the Catholic faith as the supreme teacher of the universal Church, in whom the Church's charism of infallibility is present in a singular way.

(Dogmatic Constitution on the Church par. 25)

Furthermore, when the Roman Pontiff, or the body of bishops together with him, define a doctrine, they make the definition in conformity with revelation itself, to which all are bound to adhere and to which they are obliged to submit . . .

(Dogmatic Constitution on the Church par. 25)

Magisterium in General

[Questions covered: Can the Holy Father exercise his teaching authority only in those situations where a consensus already exists among Catholics? Or can the Pope also employ his authority to settle controversial questions? Is it not only possible—but even sometimes highly desirable for the Pope to make binding decisions in areas where there has previously been internal disagreement rather than consensus?]

No matter how much the Sacred Magisterium avails itself of the contemplation, life, and study of the faithful, its office is not reduced merely to ratifying the assent already expressed by the latter. Indeed, in the interpretation and explanation of the written or transmitted word of God, the Magisterium can anticipate or demand their assent. The people of God has particular need of the intervention and assistance of the magisterium when internal disagreements arise and spread concerning a doctrine that must be believed or held, lest it lose the communion of the one faith in the one body of the Lord.

(Mysterium ecclesiae, June 1973

Ordinary Magisterium

[Questions covered: What about those occasions when the Holy Father is exercising the "ordinary magisterium" rather than the "extraordinary magisterium"—that is, when he is employing his authentic teaching authority but not speaking "ex cathedra?" Does Vatican II recognize a right of Catholics to dissent from such teachings of the "ordinary magisterium?" Or does Vatican II insist that Catholics are required to acknowledge and adhere to these teachings—and not only in some vague verbal way but in the exact way intended by the Pope?]

. . . Religious submission of will and of mind must be shown in a special way to the authentic teaching authority of the Roman Pontiff, even when he is not speaking *ex cathedra*. That is, it must be shown in such a way that his supreme Magisterium is acknowledged with reverence, the judgments made by him are sincerely adhered to, according to his manifest mind and will. His mind and will in the matter may be known chiefly either from the character of the documents, from his frequent repetition of the same doctrine, or from his manner of speaking.

(Dogmatic Constitution on the Church (par. 25)

[Questions covered: Since the Pope usually does not exercise his "extraordinary magisterium" in Papal encyclicals, is it true to say that the teaching contained in encyclicals does not in itself demand assent? Or, on the contrary, does Our Lord's promise to His disciples that "He who hears you, hears me" apply to the ordinary magisterium of the Pope? What about those theologians with special expertise in the field? Because of their knowledge, is it permissible for them to respectfully voice their dissent when the Pope in an official document purposely passes judgment on a matter debated until then?]

Nor must it be thought that what is contained in encyclical letters does not of itself demand assent, on the pretext that the Popes do not exercise in them the supreme power of their teaching authority. Rather, such teachings belong to the ordinary magisiterium, of which it is true to say: 'He who hears you, hears Me' (Lk. 10:16); For the most part, too, what is expounded and inculcated in encyclical letters already appertains to Catholic doctrine for other reasons. But if the supreme Pontiffs in official documents purposely pass judgment on a matter debated until then, it is obvious to all that the matter, according to the mind and will of the same Pontiffs, cannot be considered any longer a question open for discussion among theologians.

(Humani generis Aug 12, 1950, AAS 42)

Infallibility

In addition to emphasizing the responsibility of all Catholics to assent to the doctrinal teaching of the Holy Father (whether the teaching be from the Pope's "extraordinary magisterium" or his "ordinary magisterium"), the Second Vatican Council reaffirmed what was solemnly defined by the First Vatican Council: that the Pope can make infallible statements on faith and morals.

Infalliblity is a gift of God to His Church. There are certain times when the Church must make a decision which, if wrong, would keep Her from carrying out the mission of Jesus. In the early Church, for example, the Catholic belief that Jesus is God was attacked by some people who considered themselves to be "theological experts." Acting very much like those "theological experts" of today who challenge the Church's official teaching, the dissenters in the early Church argued strenuously against the Divinity of Jesus and tried to force the Pope and the bishops to repudiate this doctrine. Obviously, a wrong decision on this matter would have changed totally the Christian religion. "Infallibilty" means that Jesus (Who promised to be with His Church until the end of time and Who also promised that the "gates of hell" would not prevail against Her) will guide the Pope in all such situations and protect the Holy Father from any erroneous teaching that would mislead the people of God.

As the quotation from Pope Paul VI indicates, infallible statements may be made to settle a controversy. Or, as in 1950, when Pius XII defined the doctrine of Our Blessed Lady's Assumption into heaven, an infallible statement may be proclaimed in order to give added emphasis and honor to a truth already believed by the entire Church. In addition to the Pope, a General Council of the bishops may make infallible statements provided that their actions are approved by the Holy Father.

Whenever the extraordinary magisterium is employed by the Holy Father (or by a general council of the bishops with Papal approval) to make a binding decision on a matter of faith or morals, the teaching is infallible. However, as the name itself indicates, the use of the "extraordinary" magisterium is rare. The last example was the definition of the Assumption in 1950. Prior to that, the extraordinary magisterium was employed in 1870 by the First Vatican Council in defining Papal infalliblity and in 1854 by Pope Pius X in defining the Immaculate Conception of the Blessed Mother.

Because the use of the extraordinary magisterium is so dramatic, there is always the danger of overlooking the importance of the ordinary magisterium. Even the language may confuse us somewhat, since we frequently employ the word "ordinary" to refer to something that is "mediocre". (John asks Mary, "How was the Broadway play you saw last night?" "Oh," she replies, "it was just ordinary.")

That is not what the Church means in using the phrase "ordinary" magisterium. Rather, the word refers to the usual way in which something is done. If I live in Illinois, but I also have a summer home in Wyoming, then my "ordinary" residence is Illinois and my "extraordinary" residence is Wyoming. The use of these terms does not tell me anything about whether my house in Wyoming is better than my house in Illinois. All it means is that I usually live in Illinois and go to Wyoming on special occasions.

This point must be emphasized because some of those who challenge the Church's teaching claim that they accept the extraordinary magisterium but reject the ordinary magisterium. While other dissenters are somewhat more candid in admitting that they actually reject the extraordinary magisterium as well, those who say "extraordinary, yes; ordinary, no" recognize that such a position can have advantages from a public-relations viewpoint. Since the extraordinary magisterium is unlikely to be employed in their lifetime, the dissenters can still reject any statement the Pope makes. At the same time, however, they can claim to respect Church authority.

Not only is such a position opposed to the official teaching of the Church, but it is also based on the mistaken assumption that if a matter is truly important the Pope will employ the extraordinary magisterium. In reality, some of the most important statements of the Church are teachings of the ordinary magisterium.

In order to appreciate better the error involved in rejecting the Church's "ordinary" teaching and following only the "extraordinary," let us consider something else that is truly extraordinary— a miracle of God. We know that Our Lord sometimes works miracles. When He does, it is an occasion of tremendous joy.

But does this mean that God is present in our lives only when He works a miracle? Not at all. In fact, most of us will never witness such an extraordinary manifestation of God's power. Yet God loves all of us and, unless we refuse His grace, Our Lord's guidance will truly be present in our lives in ways that may be less dramatic than a miracle but will be just as real and just as important.

If a particular individual rejected the idea of God's "ordinary" presence in his life—if he announced "I believe in miracles, but outside of the miraculous, I don't believe in God's guidance"—such a person would be missing the entire meaning of what God has done for us.

The same can be said of the Church's teaching. Jesus promised Peter and the Apostles: "I am with you always; yes, to the end of time." He did not say: "I will be with you, but only on very rare occasions, perhaps one day every hundred years or so when the extraordinary magisterium is exercised." Those who deny Our Lord's guidance of His Church's "ordinary" magisterium are like those who limit the presence of God in our lives to those rare (although marvelous) occasions when a miracle takes place.

In attempting to undermine the confidence of Catholics in the teaching of the Holy Father, those who dissent often make this comment with reference to the ordinary magisterium: Statements of the ordinary magisterium are not infallible.'' The impression is carefully created by the dissenters that the Church Herself admits such teachings can be mistaken. Thus, it is argued, the teaching of the ordinary magisterium is ''uncertain.''

When the challengers of the Pope are successful in creating this impression, the effect can be devastating on those Catholics who are trying to be faithful to the Church's teaching. This is especially true in those situations where the loyal acceptance of the Pope's magisterium can involve great sacrifice (e.g., the teaching of the Holy Father on contraception). If they believe the dissenters on the ''uncertainty'' question, Catholics must inevitably think to themselves: ''Why in the world should I continue to make the sacrifices involved if the Church Herself isn't sure of what She is saying? Won't I be a fool if I struggle along this way for twenty years, and then the Church announces 'Sorry, people, it was all a mistake'?''

Because the ''uncertain'' ploy has been used so often and in such a damaging way by Church dissenters, let us consider in some detail both the certainty of the ordinary magisterium and the precise meaning of the word ''infallible.''

In claiming that teachings of the ordinary magsterium can be erroneous, the dissenters are using the word ''infallible'' as a synonym for the phrase ''extraordinary magsterium.'' The logic of their position proceeds as follows:

1. The Church has declared that *ex cathedra* statements are infallible.
2. But a teaching of the ordinary magsterium is not an *ex cathedra* statement.
3. Therefore, a teaching of the ordinary magsterium is not infallible.

To understand the logical error in such reasoning, suppose that your friend Sam Brown suddenly announces that a dog is not an animal. Astounded at this conclusion, you ask Sam for an explanation and he replies:

1. I know with certainty that cats are animals.
2. But a dog is not a cat.
3. Therefore, a dog is not an animal.

If you compare the reasoning of Sam Brown with the reasoning of those Catholics who attack the ordinary magisterium, you will find that the logical process is exactly the same. Sam jumps from the true statement that ''cats are animals'' to the false conclusion that ''only cats are animals.'' The dissenting Catholics jump from the true statement that *"ex cathedra* statements are free from error" to the false conclusion that "only *ex cathedra* statements are free from error."

It is always important to distinguish what the Church herself teaches on a subject from what people say the Church teaches, especially when the "people who say" are those who dissent from the Pope and want to downgrade the importance of the Church's official teaching. We have already seen this with respect to Vatican II, where the actual teaching of the Council about the authoirty of the Pope is very different from those false claims about the Council that are made by people who challenge the Holy Father.

Therefore, let us ask this question. Has the Church herself ever taught that the ordinary magisterium can be erroneous?

Before proceeding to an answer, it might be good to recall quickly the conditions set down in the five Church statements (on the ordinary magisterium and the extraordinary magsterium) that we quoted previously.

First, when we talk about infalliblity, we are referring to teaching on faith and morals, not to the Pope's personal views on science, art, politics or any other non-religious subject.

Second, it is the Church's "doctrine" that is involved, a teaching on faith or morals that the Church says comes from God and, therefore, must be faithfully proclaimed by the Church (as opposed to the Church's "discipline" those laws or customs that come not from God but from the Church Herself and so can be changed at will).

Third, we are referring to the Pope's *official* statements, authoritative teaching that the Holy Father has directed to the entire Church in virtue of his office as the Vicar of Christ. (Sometimes a Pope, while he has a personal opinion on a theological matter, may choose not to make it a part of his official teaching. Or the Pope, who also serves as the Bishop of Rome, may be speaking in that capacity only to his own diocese or to some other part of the Church rather than to the entire Church. In contrast with such situations, what is being considered here is the official teaching of the Holy Father to the whole Church in virtue of his office as Vicar of Christ.)

Fourth, to quote the words we saw from Pius XII, the Pope is "purposely passing judgment" on a matter of faith and morals. The Pope is dealing directly with a question and he intends to make a binding decision. There is a finality to his action.

What this last condition excludes are the many situations where the Pope does not intend to make a binding decision. A Pope is usually very careful not to settle a theological controversy until he believes there has been sufficient time for the Church to pray and reflect on the matter.

In a succeeding chapter, we will be discussing how the Church, over the course of the centuries, can advance in her appreciation and deepen her understanding of what Christ has done for us. Such growth never means that the Church reverses what she has once taught infallibly, but it does mean that, through the assistance of the Holy Spirit, the Church—sometimes after centuries of prayer and reflection—can understand more clearly what was once somewhat obscure.

Recognizing this fact, a Pope may decide that the proper time has not yet arrived to make a binding doctrinal decision. At some point that time will arrive but not at present. Nevertheless, this does not necessarily mean that the Holy Father will be silent on the subject. Without totally "closing the door" on a discussion, the Pope may believe it is important to inform the Catholic people that the Church is leaning very strongly in a particular direction and may shortly be making a binding doctrinal decision.

Another action the Holy Father may take is to make, not a doctrinal decision, but a disciplinary decision because of the pastoral needs of the Church. The Pope may say to both sides in a theological controversy: "Look, this discussion has become so hot that it is adversely affecting the peace of the Church. Therefore, without making a final decision on the doctrinal question itself, I believe it is in the best interests of the Church that you stop public discussion on this matter for the present."

Yet a third approach that the Holy Father can take is to teach in the manner that is sometimes employed by civil judges in a court case. While making a binding decision on a matter before the court, a judge will often go further and make comments referred to as *obiter dicta*. The American Heritage Dictionary defines *obiter dicta* as "passing comments, opinions voiced by a judge that have only incidental bearing on the case in question and are therefore not binding."

Like a judge, the Pope can make *obiter dicta*—non-binding statements that are intended to be of value but not to have the force of authoritative decision. That is the reason both Vatican II and Pius XII emphasize the importance of the Pope's intention. Pope Pius speaks of a Pope "purposely passing judgment" while Vatican II teaches that the Pope's decisions must be "sincerely adhered to, according to his manifest mind and will. His mind and will in the matter may be known chiefly either from the character of the documents, from his frequent repetition of the same doctrine, or from his manner of speaking."

Teachings on faith or morals, doctrine that the Holy Father judges is a divine teaching or a divine law (not disciplinary rulings or pastoral directives), teaching officially made to the entire Church in virtue of the Pope's authority as the Vicar of Christ, teaching that the Pope intends to be binding (not *obiter dicta* or any other kind of non-binding teaching)—if the ordinary magisterium is employed by the Pope under all the conditions listed above, can the teaching involved be erroneous?

What the Church Herself Teaches

When we look closely at the official statements of the Popes and the Councils on the inerrancy of the ordinary magisterium, we find the following.

1) The Church has taught that there are many occasions when the ordinary magisterium is infallible. (In other words, the Church rejects the view of the dissenters that only the extraordinary magisterium is free from error.)

2) The Church has not said—one way or the other—whether *all* statements of the ordinary magisterium are infallible. (On the one hand, the Church appears to have taken great care not to say that it is possible for a binding decision of the ordinary magisterium to be erroneous. On the other hand, the Church has not taught expressly that all such binding decisions are infallible.)

3) However, the Church has said that every Catholic has an obligation to assent to *all* the teaching of the ordinary magisterium—assuming, of course, that the Holy Father intends those teachings to be binding. The obligation to assent arises precisely because of the Church's belief that Jesus is with His Church not only on "extraordinary" occasions but also in her "ordinary" teaching. Thus, if you assume that a binding doctrinal decision of the ordinary magisterium can be erroneous, you are then faced with the difficulty of explaining why Our Lord would require Catholics to assent to such a statement (for the Church teaches both that there is such a requirement and that the ultimate source of this obligation is Christ Himself) while still allowing His Church to be in error on the subject.

Let us first consider those occasions when the Church clearly teaches that the ordinary magisterium is infallible.

The First Vatican Council made the following declaration in its *Dogmatic Constitution Concerning the Catholic Faith*:

> By divine and Catholic faith everything must be believed that is contained in the written word of God or in tradition, and that is proposed by the Church as a divinely revealed object of belief, either in a solemn decree or in her ordinary, universal magisterium.

What does the word "universal" mean? In another statement issued during his Pontificate, Pius IX, the Pope who presided over Vatican I, described "universal" as "the ordinary teaching power of the whole Church spread throughout the world."

Vatican II also taught the infallibilty of the ordinary and universal magisterium in the following statement about the teaching authority of bishops:

> Although the bishops, taken individually, do not enjoy the privilege of infallibility, they do, however, proclaim infallibly the doctrine of Christ on the following conditions: namely, when, even though dispersed throughout the world but preserving for all that among themselves and with Peter's successor the bond of commmunion, in their authoritative teaching concerning matters of faith and morals, they are in agreement that a particular teaching is to be held definitively and absolutely.

The "agreement of the bishops" referred to by Vatican II does not mean that every single bishop in the world must assent to the teaching involved. For, as Vatican II mentioned at the start of its statement, it is always possible for an individual bishop to be in error. What it does mean, however, is that there is a consensus among the bishops—a general agreement on the doctrine that is close to being unanimous. The bishops who agree on the doctrine must have a "bond of communion" with Peter's successor, which means that the Pope must share their view since, as Vatican II emphasizes, the bishops can never exercise their collective infalliblity without the approval of the Holy Father.

Pope Pius XII also stressed the infalliblity of the ordinary, universal magisterium when he defined the dogma of the Assumption of Our Blessed Lady. Pope Pius knew that some people were wondering how the Church could be certain of the Assumption since the doctrine was not explicitly mentioned in the Bible. The Pope explained that he had written to all the bishops in the Catholic Church and asked them whether they believed that the Assumption could be defined as a dogma of faith. In the Pope's own words, he received "an almost unanimous affirmative response." Therefore, quoting the teaching of Vatican I about the infallibility of the ordinary and universal magisterium, Pius XII concluded that:

> . . . from the universal agreement of the Church's ordinary teaching authority we have a certain and firm proof, demonstrating that the Blessed Virgin Mary's bodily Assumption into heaven—which surely no faculty of the human mind could know by its own natural powers, as far as the heavenly glorification of the virginal body of the loving mother of God is concerned —is a truth that has been revealed by God and

consequently something that must be firmly and faithfully believed by all children of the Church.

Notice that Pius XII did not say: "The Assumption is certainly true because the doctrine has been taught by the extraordinary magisterium." What he said was the reverse: "The Assumption can be taught by the extraordinary magsterium because we know already from the ordinary and universal magisterium that the belief is certainly true."

In summary, if at any one moment in the Church's history it can be shown that the Pope, acting through his ordinary magisterium has made a binding doctrinal decision and if it can also be demonstrated that there is a consensus among the bishops and that they have joined with the Pope in this teaching, then the doctrine can be considered infallible even if the extraordinary magisterium has not been employed.

While the fact that a binding doctrine is taught universally at any one period of time can itself be sufficient proof of its certainty, there is a second proof that is also available with respect to many Church doctrines, and that is the fact that the Church has stressed a particular belief for many centuries. In other words, just as there is a "universality" of the present, so there is "universality" of time. Pius XII employed this "argument from time" as an additional proof that the doctrine of Our Lady's Assumption was certainly true. After a thorough study of the many ways the Catholic Church had emphasized Mary's Assumption through the centuries, Pope Pius concluded:

> Since the Universal Church, within which dwells the Spirit of Truth who infallibly directs it towards an ever more perfect knoweldge of the revealed truths, has expressed its own belief many times over the course of the centuries, and since the Bishops of the entire world are almost unanimously petitioning that the truth of the bodily Assumption of the Blessed Virgin Mary into heaven should be defined as a dogma of divine and Catholic faith—this truth which is based on the Sacred Writings, which is thoroughly rooted in the minds of the faithful, which has been approved in ecclesiastical worship from the most remote times, which is completely in harmony with the other revealed truths, and which has been expounded and explained magnificently in the work, the science, and the wisdom of the theologians—we believe that the moment appointed in the plan of divine providence for the solemn proclamation of this outstanding privilege of the Virgin Mary has already arrived.

In giving us these three examples of occasions when we can be certain that Christ will protect the Church in her teaching, the Popes and Councils have carefully avoided saying that these are the only circumstances in which Jesus will keep His Church from falling into error. Therefore, it might be good to look at these three examples and ask ourselves this question: What do they have in common and why can we be certain that Christ guards His Church from error on these occasions?

The answer is that each of the three ways of teaching involves a situation of importance. The extraordinary magisterium is only exercised in circumstances that the Pope considers to be of great importance. As for the ordinary and universal magisterium, if virtually every bishop in the entire world is in agreement that a doctrinal teaching is to be held "definitively and absolutely," then this is obviously an important teaching. The same can be said of the ordinary magisterium taught through the centuries. If either the Church for hundreds of years or all the present successors of the Apostles could teach doctrinal error, then how could we say that Our Lord protects the teaching of His Church?

Because Jesus continually guides the Church He founded, there are, beyond the three occasions already mentioned, a number of other situations in which we can know with certainty that Christ has preserved the Pope's decisions from error. For example, when we considered the difference between doctrine and discipline, the statement was made that, "with one exception," infallibility does not apply to question of discipline. The exception is a simple one: No change in Church discipline can ever result in the elimination of anything basic to the Church's mission.

In the mid 1960's, for instance, Pope Paul VI approved some changes in the prayers of the Mass. While preserving the meaning and all the essential parts of the Mass, the Holy Father made some non-essential changes that he thought would help the Catholic people to understand better and to participate more devoutly in the Mass.

Question: Although the Pope's purpose was to change only non-essentials, could he have made a mistake and removed something basic? Could the Holy Father have created accidentally a situation in which the Mass was no longer the Mass—a situation in which all the Masses offered by Catholic priests under the new discipline were invalid?

No, he could not. While the Church's practical judgment about the value of a disciplinary change does not involve infalliblity there most certainly is a promise from Our Lord that whatever is fundamental to the Church's Mission will always be preserved. No disciplinary change can ever result in the removal of something essential.

The example is of current interest because some of the people who attend the "traditionalist" churches make exactly the argument discussed above—namely, that despite the intention of the Pope to change only non-essentials, he actually destroyed the Mass and created a situation in which the Mass no longer exists in a valid way within the Catholic Church. When asked how this could be, they respond: "The Pope's action wasn't infallible because it didn't involve an *ex cathedra* statement of the extraordinary magisterium."

Such people apparently assume that Our Lord is like those children who play a game in which it is permissible to tell any lie you wish as long as you have your fingers crossed. According to the children's game, if you cross your fingers behind your back, you can then break your word, no matter how serious. Why? "It doesn't matter because I had my fingers crossed."

In the same way, Our Lord is supposedly thinking in heaven: "Well, the Pope really did it that time. He just abolished the Mass and destroyed the Church. And the funny thing is he thought he was being helpful. But I don't have to do anything about it because it wasn't an *ex cathedra* statement."

Jesus does not play such games. He does not "cross his fingers."

Birth Control and the Magisterium

The traditionalists, of course, are not the only people who pretend that Christ plays games. Those who reject the Pope's teaching on contraception make a similar assumption about Our Lord.

When Pope Paul VI reaffirmed the Church's constant teaching on contraception, he acted for one reason only—because of the firm belief that it was his solemn responsibility as the Vicar of Christ to proclaim and defend the divine law. The Holy Father knew that the dissenting Catholics had carefully prepared an organized revolt if he dared to speak. He recognized that his decision would be considered a "hard saying." When Jesus Himself had made such a "hard saying" during His own lifetime, the followers of Our Lord had deserted Him in droves, and the Pope realized that the Vicar of Christ could expect no better treatment. Ultimately, however, the one and only consideration for Pope Paul VI had to be: "Is this what Jesus wants me to do?" Our Lord Himself had demonstrated that a "hard saying" could still be a "true saying." If the teaching were true—if it involved a divine law—then the Pope had the obligation to do what Christ Himself had done, to proclaim the doctrine openly and firmly, no matter what the consequences in terms of ridicule and rejection.

Those who argue glibly that the Pope could be in error because "it's not an *ex cathedra* statement of the extraordinary magisterium" are ultimately saying something not about the Pope but about Our Lord. As with the traditionalists, Christ is supposed to be thinking in heaven: "Look at that! The Pope just made a monumental mistake down there. Because he sincerely thought a divine law was involved—when it really wasn't—my Vicar on earth has imposed on millions of families an obligation that they don't really have. Furthermore, thousands of people will lose their faith because of the error made by my representative. Ironically, the Pope only made this decision because—after years of prayer and study in which he sought to know my will and to appeal to me for guidance—the Pope became convinced that this was the action I wanted.

"Now normally you might think that I should do something about this—help the Pope who is praying to me for support as he exercises the office I gave him, or help the millions of Catholics who would be hurt seriously by an erroneous teaching. But, you see, I don't have to be concerned. Why? Because it's not an *ex cathedra* statement of the extraordinary magisterium."

Once again we see the dissenters turning Christ into a player of games. No matter how crucial the decision may be for the survival of the Church, those who attack the Holy Father's teaching would have us believe that—for Jesus Christ—"it doesn't count if he has his fingers crossed."

Before leaving the question of the Church's teaching on contraception, it might be good to emphasize that, in addition to its importance, the doctrine has been taught by the ordinary and universal magisterium. That fact alone would make it an infallible teaching, since both Vatican I and Vatican II proclaim that a Church doctrine must be certainly true if at any one point in time it has been taught in a "definitive and absolute" manner by the ordinary magisterium of the Pope and the bishops throughout the world.

The Church's teaching on contraception has been taught in this way not just at one point in time but for many centuries. To cite only one example, here is what Pope Pius XI wrote in 1930 on the morality of contraception:

> But surely no reason, not even the gravest, can bring it about that what is intrinsically against nature becomes in accord with nature, and honorable. Since, moreover, the conjugal act by its very nature is destined for the generating of offspring, those who in the exercise of it deliberately deprive it of its natural force and power, act contrary to nature, and do something that is shameful and intrinsically bad . . .
>
> Since, therefore, certain persons, manifestly departing from Christian doctrine handed down from the beginning without interruption, have recently decided that another doctrine should be preached on this method of acting, the Catholic Church, to whom God himself has entrusted the teaching and the defense of the integrity and purity of morals,

placed in the midst of this ruination of morals, in order that she may preserve the chastity of the marriage contract immune from this base sin, and in token of her divine mission raises high her voice through Our mouth and again proclaims: Any use of the marriage act, in the exercise of which it is designedly deprived of its natural power of pro-creating life, infringes on the law of God and of nature and those who have committed any such act are stained with the guilt of serious sin.

Therefore, we admonish the priests who devote time to hearing con-fessions, and others who have care of souls, in accord with Our highest authority, not to permit the faithful committed to them to err in this most serious law of God, and much more to keep themselves immune from false opinions of this kind, and not to connive in them in any way. If any confessor or pastor of souls, which may God forbid, either himself leads the faithful entrusted to him in these errors, or at least either by approval or by guilty silence confirms them in these errors, let him know that he must render a strict account'ng to God, the Supreme Judge, for the betrayal of his trust, and let him consider the words of Christ as spoken to himsef: "They are blind, and the leaders of the blind; and if the blind lead the blind, both fall into the pit" (Matt 15:14).

(Pius XI, *Casti Connubi*, Dec 31, 1930)

Could any statement of the ordinary magisterium be more "absolute and definitive?" Pius XI teaches explicitly that contraception violates a "most serious law of God" and that the Church, in virtue of her "divine mission," must proclaim again what she has taught through the ages. In accord with the Pope's "highest authority," the Holy Father binds priests to teach this doctrine, and he warns them that, if they do otherwise, they will be guilty before "God, the Supreme Judge, for the betrayal of his trust."

As for universality, the active support of bishops throughout the world can be demonstrated historically without the shadow of a doubt. Not only did the bishops join with the Pope in emphasizing the importance of this moral question, but their backing of the doctrine was as universal as the teaching itself was definitive. And this situation existed not only in 1930 but throughout the centuries. To quote Piux XI directly, the Church's posi-tion on contraception is a "Christian doctrine handed down from the begin-ning without interruption."

Therefore, those Catholic couples who have made such heroic sacrifices to remain faithful to the Church's teaching should not be concerned that the doctrine may change. They should never allow themselves to be tricked by the dissenters into believing that the Church is uncertain. They should also know that God loves them in a very special way for the faith they have shown and the sacrifices they have made.

It is only natural to want to avoid sacrifice. Christ Himself felt that way in the Garden of Gethsemane. At the same time, however, Our Lord was determined at all costs to remain faithful to the Will of His Father.

In a similar spirit, Catholic couples should learn about the reliable and greatly improved methods of natural family planning, since this provides a way to remain faithful to the divine law while eliminating much of the personal hardship that is involved. Nevertheless, to the extent that loyalty to Jesus still demands sacrifice, Catholic families who are faithful to the Church's teaching should always remember one thing:

The cross of Christ has never been popular, and in our own age this is especially true. There are many who sincerely want to follow Jesus, but there are only a few who are willing to suffer with Him and to stand under His Cross. Those few, however, have a special place in God's Kingdom. They share Christ's Resurrection according to the way they have shared His Crucifixion.

5.
The Use of Words

Suppose I were to start this chapter with the following comment: "A statement can be infallible without being infallible."

I suspect the reaction of many readers would be: "What sort of crazy gibberish is that? Has he taken leave of his senses?"

Nevertheless, the comment can be true, if it is understood properly. In the same way, here are three other statements that are also true, if they are understood properly:

(1) A person can be an authority without being an authority.

(2) An athlete can be disciplined without being disciplined.

(3) Something can be ordinary without being ordinary.

Double talk? Not really. What we actually have is "double meaning." These four words—infallible, authority, discipline, and ordinary—are all words that can be used in more than one way.

With the exception of the word "infallible," we have already discussed the double meaning of these words. In previous sections, we considered how the word "authority" can refer either to "an expert" or to "an office-holder." The word "discipline" can mean either "training" or "punishment," while the word "ordinary" can be used as a synonym for "mediocre" or for "usual."

Therefore:

(1) A person can be an authority (in the sense of "expert") without being an authority (in the sense of "office-holder").

(2) An athlete can be disciplined (in the sense of "trained" without being disciplined (in the sense of "punished").

(3) Something can be ordinary (in the sense of "usual") without being ordinary (in the sense of "mediocre").

Notice what a tremendously different impression the three sentences create on us when a parenthesis is added to alert us to the fact that a word is being used in two different ways. What seemed absurd and nonsensical without a parenthesis becomes quite believable with the proper clarification.

In discussing Church matters, it is important for Catholics to keep in mind the various usages of a word. Sometimes a word will have a popular meaning, but the Church employs it in a more restricted and technical sense. Sadly, a favorite strategy of Church dissenters is to attempt to capitalize on this situation. By deliberatley using words in a vague way or in a manner different from that intended by the Church, the dissenters hope either to discredit a Church teaching or to confuse people about its actual meaning. While this amounts to a form of trickery against the Catholic people, those seeking to undermine the Pope are more concerned about effectiveness than about ethics.

Since "infallible" is a word with different meanings, and since Church dissenters have often used the word in a misleading way, let us study this word more closely to see whether—surprising as it may seem—a statement can be infallible without being infallible.

The Three Meanings of Infallible

Although the word "infallible" always has the basic meaning of "free from error," the word can be used in a broad and general manner, or in a more restricted manner, or, finally, in a most restricted manner. As we define these three ways below, we will underline the new part of the definition that is added to each way.

A) Broad, General Meaning: *any statement that is certainly true*

B) More Restricted Meaning (Catholic Church): any statement that is certainly true *because of the guidance of the Holy Spirit*

C) Most Restricted Meaning (Catholic Church): any statement that is certainly true because of the guidance of the Holy Spirit *and that has been proclaimed as such by the extraordinary magisterium*

Can you and I make infallible statements? Certainly. If you say that John Kennedy was once the President of the United States, or that Tuesday is the English name of the day that follows Monday, or that you are reading this sentence at the present moment, you are making statements that are certainly true. To claim that such statements might be erroneous would be to deny the very foundations of knowledge itself.

The more restricted meaning of infallibility refers to statements that are guided by the Holy Spirit. As discussed in the last chapter, this category would certainly include the teachings of the extraordinary magisterium, the teachings of the ordinary and universal magisterium, and other decisions of the Pope that, if erroneous, would seriously mislead the people of God or result in the elimination of something basic from the Church.

Sometimes the word "infallible" is used in a more technical sense to refer only to acts of the extraordinary magisterium. In other words, "infallible" is employed like the phrase "ex cathedra." As we saw in the last chapter, "ex cathedra" can be translated as "official." Nevertheless, while both the ordinary magisterium and the extraordinary magisterium are official, the use of the phrase "ex cathedra" is restricted to the extraordinary magisterium. The phrase takes on a technical meaning that is narrower than its literal translation.

This can also be the case with "infallible," especially when phrases like "an infallible definition" or "an infallible statement" are involved. When used in this way, the question, "Is it an infallible definition?" means "Is it an act of the extraordinary magisterium?"

Suppose that you have a friend who is a bishop. Feeling in an impish mood one day, you decide to have a little fun with your friend.

The bishop is in his study watching the news on television. Entering the room, you ask the bishop what he is doing. Naturally enough, the bishop replies, "I'm watching the news on television." Then you inquire of the bishop: "What were the major new stories today?" He responds with all the detail that you desire.

Ten minutes later you turn the topic to Vatican II. Did the Council teach that the Pope as an individual can make infallible statements? "Yes," answered the bishop. Well, did the Council teach that a bishop as an individual can make infallible statements? "No," says your friend, "an individual bishop cannot make an infallible statement."

That's all you wanted to hear. "Now I've got you!", you announce to your friend. "You yourself are an individual bishop. You've just stated flatly that an individual bishop cannot make an infallible statement. Therefore, by your own words, you've admitted the possibility that everything you've said since I came into the room could be in error. For example, you're conceding that you could be mistaken in saying that you are watching television in the study. For all you know, you could actually be fifty miles away swimming in the ocean."

Rushing outside, you immediately inform the bishop's friends: "Guess what! I just had at talk with the bishop while he was watching television in his study. He admitted that he's not sure whether he is in the study, or fifty miles away. He's also not sure whether he is watching television or swimming in the ocean."

After a few moments, you would probably confess your little joke. However, if you did not—and if the bishop's friends believed your report— their confidence in the bishop's mental ability would be seriously undermined. They would conclude that, for some unexplained reason, the bishop had suddenly gone out of his mind.

How were the bishop's friends misled? By means of a word-trick involving "infallible." In actuality, when the bishop stated that he could not make an infallible statement, he had no intention whatever of conceding the possiblity that he might be in error about where he was or what he was doing. The opposite impression was created by deliberately failing to explain that a statement can be infallible (in the sense of "certainly true") without being infallible (in the sense of "an exercise of the Church's extraordinary magisterium").

The process by which the bishop's friends were tricked is the same process that Church dissenters employ in their attempt to deceive the Catholic people. In both cases, the first step is to try to induce a Church authority to use the word "infallible" in the restricted and technical sense, to say "It's not an infallible statement" meaning "It's not a statement of the extraordinary magisterium." If this can be accomplished, then the next step is to misinterpret deliberately. The Catholic people are informed: "See, Church authority itself admits the teaching can be in error."

In case the dissenters ever attempt to pull this trick in your presence, remember that the Church has taught expressly that it is not only the extraordinary magisterium but also the ordinary, universal magisterium that is protected from error by the Holy Spirit. As for the word "infallible," the story of the bishop in his study can provide an easy way to recall that a statement can be infallible (either in the general sense of "certainly true" or in the more restricted sense of "certainly true because of the guidance of the Holy Spirit") without being infallible (in the technical sense of the extraordinary magisterium).

(By the way, once the tricks of the dissenters are understood, you can easily catch them in their own word-games. If they pretend that "infallible" has only one meaning—and if they insist that only the extraordinary magisterium is infallible—then ask them this question: "What about the statements you yourself have just made about infalliblity? Are your own statements infallible?"

If they say "Yes," then you respond: "Well, your statements don't belong to the extraordinary magisterium. By insisting your comments are infallible, you've destroyed your own argument that only statements of the extraordinary magisterium are free from error."

If they say "No," then you respond: "Under your own logic, you've just admitted that you could be totally wrong when you say that only statements of the extraordinary magisterium are infallible. This means that you're not sure of your own statements.''

It should be noted, of course, that such responses to the dissenters are based on their own assumption that there is only one meaning to the word ''infallible.'' The assumption itself is false. Nevertheless, since the reasoning involved in the responses is exactly the same as the reasoning employed by the dissenters to attack the Church, the responses demontrate well that the logic of the dissenters is nonsense and that their arguments can actually be used to discredit anything, including their own position.)

Other Words and Other Tricks

As we end these few pages on words, it should be stressed that in addition to the four examples cited about (authority, infallible, discipline, and ordinary) our langauge contains thousands of other words that have two or more meanings. In fact, if we were to spend an afternoon browsing through a dictionary, we would encounter numerous words that have eight or ten meanings. (As one example, the American Heritage Dictionary lists eleven different meanings for the word ''freedom.'') Often the multiple meanings of a word are related. Nevertheless, each meaning is also ''different'' in some respect, which is the reason it is listed under a different number in the dictionary.

Because so many words have multiple meanings, those who wish to discredit the official teaching of the Church have many opportunities to use a word or a phrase in a different manner from the meaning intended by the Church. Furthermore, this is only one of several tricks that the dissenters can play. In a previous section, we discussed the difference between doctrinal statements of the Church and disciplinary statements, between direct statements and ''obiter dicta,'' between a final, authoritative Church decision that is intended to be binding and a provisional statement that is intended to show the Church's preference but not in a final and binding way. In their eagerness to convince the Catholic people that the Church's doctrinal teaching can be erroneous, the dissenters have often presented disciplinary statements as doctrinal statements, or ''obiter dicta'' as binding decisions, or provisional teachings as teachings intended to be final. Having created this confusion, the next step is to ''prove'' that the Church has made some errors. In reality, the alleged errors refer to matters of discipline, provisional teaching, and ''obiter dicta''—areas where infalliblity is not involved. Nevertheless, by creating the false impression that such matters belong to the Church's doctrinal teaching—and a doctrinal teaching that is direct and final—the dissenters believe they can damage the Pope's credibility on questions of faith and morals.

In the course of this work, I have tried to alert the reader to many of the deceptions employed by the dissenters. Once people know how these tricks are performed, there is little chance that such maneuvers will be successful in undermining the confidence of Catholics in the Pope and his teaching.

When they try to deceive the Catholic people by word-games and other tricks, the dissenters are operating much like stage magicians. Both are basically in the business of creating illusions. The magician appears to saw his assistant in half—"before your very eyes." The dissenter appears to show the Church contradicting Herself or looking foolish "before your very eyes." The magician makes objects vanish, no matter how big. (I recently saw a magician who made an entire airplane disappear.) The dissenter makes Church doctrines vanish, no matter how basic.

When we see a magician in action, we usually have no idea how his tricks are performed. Nevertheless, we know the most important thing of all, that they are tricks rather than reality.

Similarly, even if we do not know how the dissenters are working their illusions, we should always keep in mind that they are illusions. As "the devil can quote Scripture for his purpose," so the dissenters can quote Church documents for their purposes. Never take such quotes at face value. No matter what those who challenge the teaching and authority of the Pope appear to be "proving," know that it is actually as much of a trick as the apparent sawing of a person in half. With such knowledge, we should not be intimidated either by those who pretend to make airplanes disappear or by those who pretend to make Church doctrines vanish.

6.
The Development of Doctrine

In this chapter we will consider something that is often referred to as "the development of doctrine." Perhaps a better term would be "the development of the Church's understanding of doctrine," since a principal Church belief is that all doctrine comes from Christ and the Church Herself adds nothing new. As in the previous sections, let us begin by seeing what the official Church has taught on the subject.

Vatican I

For the doctrine of faith which God revealed has not been handed down as a philosophic invention to the human mind to be perfected, but has been entrusted as a divine deposit to the Spouse of Christ, to be faithfully guarded and infallibly interpreted. Hence, also, that understanding of its sacred dogmas must be perpetually retained, which Holy Mother Church has once declared; and there must never be recession from that meaning under the specious name of a deeper understanding. 'Therefore . . . let the understanding, the knowledge, and wisdom of individuals as of all, of one man as of the whole Church, grow and progress strongly with the passage of the ages and the centuries; but let it be solely in its own genus, namely in the same dogma, with the same sense and the same understanding.'
(Chapter 4, Dogmatic Constitution Concerning the Catholic Faith)

Vatican II

The Tradition that comes from the apostles makes progress in the Church, with the help of the Holy Spirit. There is a growth in insight into the realities and words that are being passed on. This comes about in various ways. It comes through the contemplation and study of believers who ponder these things in their hearts (cf Lk. 2:19 and 51). It comes from the intimate sense of spiritual realities which they experience. And it comes from the preaching of those who have received, along with their right of succession in the episcopate, the sure charism of truth. Thus, as the centuries go by, the Church is always advancing towards the plenitude of divine truth, until eventually the words of God are fulfilled in her. . . .

Sacred Tradition and sacred Scripture make up a single sacred deposit of the Word of God, which is entrusted to the Church. By adhering to it the entire holy people, united to its pastors, remains always faithful to the teaching of the apostles, to the brotherhood, to the breaking of bread and the prayers (cf. Acts 2:42 Greek). So, in maintaining, practicing and professing the faith that has been handed on there should be a remarkable harmony between the bishops and the faithful.

But the task of giving an authentic interpretation of the Word of God, whether in its written form or in the form of Tradition, has been entrusted to the living teaching office of the Church alone. Its authority in this matter is exercised in the name of Jesus Christ. Yet this Magisterium is not superior to the Word of God, but is its servant. It teaches only what has been handed on to it. At the divine command and with the help of the Holy Spirit, it listens to this devotedly, guards it with dedication and expounds it faithfully. All that it proposes for belief as being divinely revealed is drawn from this single deposit of faith.

(Chapter 2, Dogmatic Constitution on Divine Revelation)

In the quotation from Vatican I, it should be noted that the last sentence is itself a quote. Vatican I is making its own a statement that was originally made in the 5th century by St. Vincent of Lerins. In recent years, with full knowledge of the way some Catholics have falsely used ''development'' as an excuse for rejecting doctrine, the Church has emphasized Saint Vincent's teaching on this matter by taking an extensive quotation from him and making it a part of the Divine Office—the official prayer of the Church that all priests are expected to pray. Therefore, since both Vatican I and the current Church have gone out of their way to highlight St. Vincent on this question, let us look at the full statement that appears in the Divine Office.

Saint Vincent of Lerins

Is there to be no development of religion in the Church of Christ? Certainly, there is to be development and on the largest scale.

Who can be so grudging to men, so full of hate for God, as to try to prevent it? But it must truly be development of the faith, not alteration of the faith. Development means that each thing expands to be itself, while alteration means that a thing is changed from one thing into another.

The understanding, knowledge, and wisdom of one and all, of individuals as well as of the whole Church, ought then to make great and vigorous progress with the passing of the ages and the centuries, but only along its own line of development, that is, with the same doctrine, the same meaning and the same import.

The religion of souls should follow the law of development of bodies. Though bodies develop and unfold their component parts with the passing of the years, they always remain what they were. There is a great difference between the flower of childhood and the maturity of age, but those who become old are the very same people who were once young. Though the condition and appearance of one and the same individual may change, it is one and the same nature, one and the same person.

The tiny members of unweaned children and the grown members of young men are still the same members. Men have the same number of limbs as children. Whatever develops at a later age was already present in seminal form; there is nothing new in old age that was not already latent in childhood.

There is no doubt, then, that the legitimate and correct rule of development, the established and wonderful order of growth, is this: in older people the fullness of years always bring to completion those members and forms that the wisdom of the Creator fashioned beforehand in their earlier years.

If, however, the human form were to turn into some shape that did not belong to its own nature, or even if something were added to the sum of its members or subtracted from it, the whole body would necessarily perish or become grotesque or at least be enfeebled. In the same way, the doctrine of the Christian religion should properly follow these laws of development, that is, by becoming firmer over the years, more ample in the course of time, more exalted as it advances in age.

In ancient times our ancestors sowed the good seed in the harvest field of the Church. It would be very wrong and unfitting if we, their descendants, were to reap, not the genuine wheat of truth but the intrusive growth of error.

On the contrary, what is right and fitting is this: there should be no inconsistency between first and last, but we should reap true doctrine from the growth of true teaching, so that when, in the course of time, those first sowings yield an increase it may flourish and be tended in our day also.

As we study these quotations, it becomes clear that the Church is stressing two things. First, as the Apostles themselves understood better what Jesus had said and done as they lived their faith through the years, so the Church can grow in understanding through the centuries under the guidance of the Holy Spirit. Second, this growth never means a reversal of what has been previously taught by the Church to be divinely revealed. On the contrary, the responsibility of the Church is to preserve faithfully and forever the doctrinal teaching of Jesus.

In considering how development occurs, St. Vincent gives us the example of a child growing into a man. There is great physical progress but it is always the same person. Furthermore, what we see later in a developed form was always present from the beginning in an undeveloped way. (It is interesting that the modern science of genetics has confirmed this view of the fifth century saint. Modern science teaches that at the first moment of conception there is already present a "genetic blueprint" that determines the individual's height, sex, color of hair and eyes, and other physical characteristics.)

In summary, development should never be confused with alteration. If a boy grows up and becomes a man, that's development. If a boy grows up and becomes an elephant, that alteration.

Although the example of bodily development is a good one, some people might still say: "I can understand the growth of the human body. That's something physical. But when you are talking about a non-physical thing such as knowledge, isn't it a contradiction to say that a doctrine was always there but that people didn't know for a long time?"

Perhaps the simple example of a crossword puzzle can help us to understand what the Church is saying about her own knowledge. In considering this example, we will give a title to each of the elements that are involved in the solving of a puzzle and then we will see how the same elements exist in the Church's development of understanding.

In a crossword puzzle, all the words are present at the first moment we see it. The person who created the puzzle does not come along and add new words as we are working on it. (Permanence)

Nevertheless, although everything is present at the beginning, it may still take us a long, long time to solve the puzzle. (Development of understanding)

Of course, some puzzles may be so easy that the solver can unravel them immediately. Others may be so difficult that no progress at all can be made.

For the sake of our example, however, let us assume that you have been given a puzzle that is neither ridiculously simple nor impossibly hard. How would you go about solving it? As you begin, there will probably be some words in the puzzle that you know immediately. Often these will be words that involve an area where you have special knowledge. If you are a baseball fan, and the puzzle gives you the information that the eight letter word in "24 Across" is the last name of a Yankee centerfielder who hit safely in 56 consecutive games, then you can write "DiMaggio" in the appropriate space. Somebody who knew little about baseball could not make such progress, but you can. (Human ability)

On the other hand, if you are not an expert in medicine, you will be stumped by the 12 letter word in "8 Down," the name of the medical condition in which the bones soften because of a defiency of Vitamin D. Your brother Don, who is a doctor, would know this word, but you do not.

In addition to your background and experience, there is another factor that will affect your ability to understand what is before you. Because there are many words involved, you cannot focus on all aspects of the puzzle at the same time. If you start by concentrating on the upper left section of the puzzle, you will not be able to give similar attention to the other sections until later. Thus, there may well be a considerable period of time in which much progress has been made in the upper part of the puzzle but relatively little has been done in the lower half. (Concentration)

Once you have filled in all the words of the puzzle that you know immediately, how do you make additional progress? Basically there are two ways. First, the words are interconnected. As a result, the words you know reveal a part of the words you do not know, and what is revealed in this way often enables you to make additional progress. (Interconnection)

The second way of advancing is more difficult to describe, but many people who work crossword puzzles have experienced it. Sometimes you appear to be making no progress at all. You have looked at an unknown word many times without success. Yet you look again — and suddenly, unexpectedly, the right word flashes into your mind. You have no idea how it came to you or why you know it now when you did not previously. Without any conscious reasoning on your part, you have made a sudden leap forward in understanding. (Intuition)

Finally, besides your individual talents, there is one other thing you can do to solve the puzzle. You can ask other people for help. If your family joins you in working on the puzzle, you can benefit from the special insight of each person.

However, such assistance is not an unmixed blessing. Once the puzzle involves a group effort, disputes are likely to arise. While you are convinced that a particular word is the right answer for "36 Across," your brother insists on another word, and your sister disagrees with both of you. The debate is vehement because you all know the importance of the right word. A correct answer will be an enormous step forward, but an incorrect answer could lead you far astray.

What you are actually facing is not one problem but two. The first problem is the dispute itself. Unless there is a way to settle such controversies, the bickering and confusion could go on and on. You certainly won't solve the puzzle that way. (The need for a way to settle controversy)

On the other hand, it doesn't help at all to reach a general agreement if what you are agreeing on is the wrong answer. That would only push you deeper into error. Therefore, the second problem is to find the one way out of many that leads to the truth. (The need to arrive at the truth)

Applicability to Church Doctrine

Each of the elements described above is also applicable to the Church as she grows in her understanding of what Jesus has done for us. Thus, similar to what was said about you and the puzzle, the following statements can be made about the Church:

(1) *Permanence*: The Church does not add anything new.

(2) *Development*: However, under the guidance of the Holy Spirit, the Church develops (or, to use another phrase, makes explicit) what was always present in an undeveloped or implicit way.

(3) *Human ability*: God works through human beings, not against them. He wants us to employ the talents given to us. As applied to development, this means that the Church can be helped to grow in understanding by the ability and experience of her members. (This presumes, of course, that such human ability is being used in the service of God's Word, and not to create dissension within the Church or to substitute the gifted person's individual views for the teaching of Jesus. If this latter is the case, then the Church suffers rather than benefits.)

(4) *Concentration*: Not everything is developed at once. In God's plan, each age of the Church concentrates on certain aspects of the Divine Revelation, leaving to succeeding ages the development of other parts.

(5) *Interconnection of Doctrine*: Because the teachings of Jesus are related to each other, a development in understanding of one doctrine will also give

the Church additional insight into a number of other doctrines. Thus, every step forward by the Church creates a situation in which further advances in understanding are possible.

(6) *Intuition*: Like the solver of a puzzle, the Church can sometimes experience a sudden leap forward in understanding an unexpected advance that was not the result of any logical process. In this way, what may have been obscure for a long time can suddenly become clear.

(7) *The Need for a Way to Settle Controversy and The Need to Arrive at the Truth (The Two Roles of Authority)*: With respect to development, the Church's "magisterium," the authority of the Pope and of the bishops united with the Pope, fulfills two important functions. First, it has a *disciplinary* role. Authority provides the order within the Church that is necessary for the process of development to take place. Without the proper order, confusion could never be dispelled and disputes could never be resolved.

Second, authority has a *doctrinal* role. Acting under the guidance and protection of the Holy Spirit, Church authorities can guarantee the truth of a development in understanding. Without such a guarantee, there would be no way of knowing whether a development was true or false, whether the people of God were deepening their knowledge of the teachings of Jesus or leading themselves farther and farther away.

Although the understanding of Church doctrine is far more profound than the understanding of a crossword puzzle, the similarities we have described are quite real. Perhaps that is the reason the same word— "mystery"—is employed both with puzzles and with Church doctrines. An Agatha Christie detective story is referred to as a "mystery". At the same time, we also speak of the Joyful, Sorrowful, and Glorious "Mysteries" of the Rosary, that is, the Crucifixion, the Resurrection, and the other "mysteries" of our faith.

Church doctrines are called "mysteries" because we can never fully understand them. The basic reason for this is that such doctrines come from God and speak to us about God's Life and His relationship with us. Since God is infinite, He is beyond the complete grasp of our human understanding. Nevertheless, because of God's free decision to give Himself to us, we can have a true knowledge of God. But we know only in part, never completely. There is always something that remains hidden, something more to be discovered. This means that, through God's grace, it is always possible both for individuals and for the entire Church to advance in knowledge of the Divine.

How does such growth take place? By prayer, study, and experience, a process that must always be under the direction of the Holy Spirit in order to produce a genuine development of understanding.

While we have been stressing the similarities between the solving of a puzzle and the understanding of Church doctrine, the last few paragraphs have also given us two important differences. First, unlike a crossword puzzle, the process of understanding our faith is not just an intellectual exercise. In order to understand the divine mysteries, what is needed above all is supernatural faith and love, a gift of God Himself. The Church and her members grow in the knowledge of Christ in the same way that a loving wife grows in the knowledge of her husband.

Second, the process involved is endless. Since a crossword puzzle has only a certain number of words, it can be finished. When we read the last page of the Agatha Christie detective story, we know everything, and it is no longer a "mystery" for us. In contrast, the Resurreciton of Our Lord will always be a mystery. There will never be a moment when any follower of Jesus will be able to say: "I understand fully all that God the Father has done for us in raising His Son from the dead."

When we reflect upon the fact that the Church's knowledge of Jesus is never complete, we can see the reason that an infallible teaching authority is necessary to guarantee the legitimacy of Church development. With respect to things that can be finished, we can often know that a development is genuine by the end result. How can you be certain that you were on the right track in solving a crossword puzzle? Only by arriving at a final stage in which all the words fit together properly. How did scientists know that they were proceeding correctly in building a plane that could fly? Only by arriving at a final stage in which a plane was completed and launched successfully into the air. In both cases, "the proof is in the pudding." A successful final result gives us conclusive evidence that the development is genuine. An unsuccessful result sends us back to the drawing-board in a search for the correct answer. If we could not test the validity of our theories in this way, we would never know whether we had reached the truth. The whole process of development would then be useless.

Now the verification procedure described above does not completely work with Church doctrine. True, we can sometimes spot an error by its incompatibility with other known truths, or by its bad results (" By their fruits shall you know them."), but, while this verifiability procedure would certainly work for God (who sees all interconnections and can assess all consequences), it will not work with certainty for us. Unlike an airplane or a crossword puzzle, therefore, there is no practical way to test a doctrine by its completed result. However, there is one other way to guarnatee the truth of a development—an infallible teaching authority. That is the way Christ has chosen for His Church.

In order to appreciate how useless the process of development becomes when there is neither a guiding authority nor the ability to test, let us consider an interesting experiment that occurred a few years ago. A number of writers had decided to work together on the same story. It was a mystery novel, and all the clues were to be found in the first three chapters. Under the rules devised by the writers, the authors of the first part of the book were not to tell their colleagues the ending that they had in mind. Instead, the other writers were to deduce the correct ending from the clues and then "develop" the story. Proceeding in turn, each subsequent writer composed a chapter that contained additional clues to the solution. In an appendix to the book, the authors revealed the clues they had placed in their chapter and the solution to which these clues were intended to lead, but this section could not be read by the other writers until the entire work was finished.

How did the experiment turn out? Invariably, the writers who came later made an ingenious development of the material presented to them. Nine times out of ten, however, the development was not a correct one. With the best of intentions, the later writers misinterpreted the earlier material. Frequently what they considered to be a vital clue was actually a meaningless event, while the real clue slipped by unnoticed. The writer of chapter 8, for instance was confident that he knew the intentions of the authors of Chapters 4, 5, 6 and 7. He was wrong all four times, yet his solution was as clever as theirs.

Of course, none of this matters very much if it is only a detective story that is involved. If their tale is interesting, who really cares whether the later mystery writers ended up with a totally different story instead of developing the original? When we come to the teachings of Jesus, however, faithfulness to the original message is essential. We need God's truth, not an ingenious but false substitute. Therefore, if we are to have development at all, there must be an infallible teaching authority to guide us.

But is development really needed? Why shouldn't it be sufficient simply to read the Bible and follow the words of Jesus?

The answer lies in the free choice of God. Our Lord could have taught in many ways. If God desired, everything could have been revealed in a fully developed form from the very beginning. Then there would have been no process by which the Church grows in understanding through the ages.

While Jesus had an infinite number of possibilites open to Him, He actually chose a way that involved the process of development. Both the history of the Church and the teaching of the Church demonstrate that God's people can grow in their understanding of what Christ has revealed.

Although God's decision with respect to development was a totally free one, we can see a good reason for it when we consider the very different situations that have confronted Christ's followers in the course of the centuries. Instead of telling His Apostles about a particular situation that might not exist for a thousand years, Jesus chose to set up a teaching authority that would address these problems when they actually occurred.

For example, if one were to list the major social problems of the 1980's, the list would include both Communism and nuclear weapons. If, back in the first century, Our Lord had chosen to speak personally about all the important problems Christians would face, instead of establishing a Church whose teaching authority would address these problems as they arose, then Our Lord would have had to take Peter and the other Apostles aside and speak to them like this:

"Now, Peter, I must talk to you about Communism. This is something that will not exist for 1800 years, so you yourself would normally need to know nothing about it. Nevertheless, I have to explain it to you in order that my followers in the 20th century will be certain of God's will on this matter. To discuss Communism with you, I must teach you about another economic system called capitalism, although capitalism, like communism, will not exist for many centuries. To understand either of these economic systems, you must also learn about many of the social changes that will take place in the next 1500 years—changes in the way money is used within society—even changes in the state itself, for the kind of government that will exist in later centuries is very different from the government that exists now.

"In addition, I must teach you about nuclear weapons. In the 20th century, a major social problem will be the ability of men to drop powerful explosive devices from airplanes.

(At this point Peter asks what airplanes are.)

"Airplanes are flying machines that will come into existence at the beginning of the 20th century when two Americans will make a successful flight.

(At this point Peter asks who Americans are, since that land will not be discovered until 1492.)

The purpose of the proceeding example is not to be humorous but to illustrate the reason that Jesus may have chosen to operate as He did. Why bother Peter and the other Apostles with detailed explanations of situations they themselves would never encounter? They had enough problems with the Roman Empire of their day.

Another way of saying this is that, because Our Lord is God, Jesus possesses a power that the ordinary founder of a society does not have. The ordinary founder is not able to guide his followers after he has died. Therefore, if such a founder wants his disciples to know his will, he must try to anticipate future situations and give very detailed instructions before he dies. Otherwise, his followers will have to guess what the founder would have done, and their guess could well be wrong.

Jesus is not burdened with the limitations of ordinary founders. He can be as present to the current successor of Peter as He was to Peter himself, and Our Lord has guaranteed that He will be so present. For that reason, instead of anticipating future sitations and giving detailed instructions about them, Our Lord chose another way. During the years He lived in Judea and Galilee, Jesus concentrated on the problems that were faced by His followers at that time. Through the magisterium of the Church that He established, Jesus now speaks to us about the problems of our time. Some of these problems are the same as those faced by the Apostles, but others are different. In applying Our Lord's teaching to a situation, the Church can be said to "develop" that teaching, but it is a process that is always guided by Jesus Himself.

Two Acceptable Theories of Development

We have already seen how strongly the Church emphasizes that she has no power of her own to create doctrine. On the contrary, all her doctrines come from Our Lord. Furthermore, the Church teaches that God's Revelation was completed with the Apostolic Age. In other words, the personal coming of Jesus is God's supreme gift to us. Just as new words are not added to a crossword puzzle after its formation (although a person can make great advances in the understanding of what is already there), so new truths are not revealed to the Church after her formation (although the Church can make great advances in the understanding of what is already there).

When we study the Bible, it becomes clear that many important doctrines were emphasized by the Apostles from the very beginning of their ministry. The Resurrection of Jesus is a good example. The belief that Our Lord has truly risen from the dead is central to the preaching of the Apostles. As St. Paul writes in the Bible:

> If there is no resurrection of the dead, Christ himself cannot have been raised, and if Christ has not been raised then our preaching is useless: indeed, we are shown up as witnesses who have committed perjury before God, because we swore in evidence before God that he raised

Christ to life. . . . If our hope in Christ has been for this life only, we are the most unfortunate of all people. But Christ has in fact been raised from the dead, the first fruits of all who have fallen asleep. (I Corinthians 15:14-16, 19-21)

Doctrines such as the Resurrection are taught expressly in the New Testament. However, the Church also teaches doctrines that are not mentioned expressly in the Bible. A good example would be the doctrines of Mary's Assumption and her Immaculate Conception. With respect to these beliefs, the Church teaches as an article of divine faith that they are not only true but have been revealed by God. What the Church has not yet taught us, however, is the precise way in which God revealed these truths. In other words, that these doctrines are revealed by God is certain, and this, after all, is the most important consideration. But how these doctrines are revealed by God—whether explicitly or implicitly—is at present uncertain, and this means that there are two possible explanations, both of which are acceptable to the Church and either of which may be held by a Catholic.

The first explanation is that doctrines such as the Immaculate Conception and the Assumption are revealed explicitly by God but are found in Tradition rather than in Sacred Scripture. The second explanation is that doctrines such as the Immaculate Conception and the Assumption are truly revealed by God, but implicitly rather than explicitly. An implicitly revealed truth is a belief that is not mentioned expressly but is contained within another truth that is mentioned expressly.

All of this may sound quite complicated. Nevertheless, because of the confusion created by Church dissenters, it is important to understand it. Let us begin by presenting an example to clarify the difference between an explicit revelation and an implicit revelation.

Suppose that one morning Mrs. Doyle decides to go shopping. Immediately prior to leaving her house, she has baked a chocolate cake for her husband. Since the two of them live alone, her husband is the only person in the house when she leaves.

Two hours later, as she is returning to her house, Mrs. Doyle sees the mailman, who has just finished delivering the letters on her street. She stops to talk to the mailman, and he tells hers: "I just met your husband, Mrs. Doyle. He looks very well." *Question*: Did the mailman reveal to Mrs. Doyle that he had met her husband? Yes, and he did so explicilty. He told her this truth in so many words.

On the other hand, suppose that, without mentioning her husband at all, the mailman had said the following: "Mrs. Doyle, I just want you to know that I've had some good chocolate cakes in my lifetime, but the cake you made this morning is the best I've ever tasted." *Question*: Did the mailman reveal to Mrs. Doyle that he had met her husband? Yes—but not explicitly, since he never mentioned the fact directly. Nevertheless, from what he does reveal, Mrs. Doyle knows for certain that the mailman has been in communication with her husband. This truth is revealed implicitly in the mailman's statement about the cake.

If we develop this example a little more, we can arrive at an even closer parallel with the Church's situation. Suppose that Mrs. Doyle, in a letter to a friend, quotes directly the mailman's statement about the cake. Although this is the only comment of the mailman that she quotes, she tells her friend that there are many other things that the mailman said which she is not quoting. Finally she informs her friend that the mailman's conversation revealed to her that he had met her husband. Since Mrs. Doyle has not told her friend the precise way that the mailman revealed this fact to her, the friend could think: "It was probably revealed to Mrs. Doyle in a part of the conversation she did not write down. After all, she herself has said that there were many parts of the conversation that she did not record."

However, there is one other possibility. The friend could also think: "While the mailman might have revealed this truth to Mrs. Doyle in an unrecorded part of their conversation, it isn't necessary to believe this in order to accept the fact that the mailman revealed that he had met her husband. What Mrs. Doyle wrote down—namely, the mailman's comment about the cake—reveals quite clearly, although implicitly, that the mailman had met her husband."

As we apply all this to the Church, let us begin with the first explanation, that Jesus could have revealed doctrines that are not contained in the Bible. Is there any evidence to support such a position?

In the Gospel according to St. John, the Apostle faithfully records many of the sayings and actions of Jesus. Nevertheless, St. John concludes his Gospel with the following words: "There were many other things that Jesus did; if all were written down, the world itself, I suppose, would not hold all the books that would have to be written."

Since St. John's Gospel is a part of the Bible, Sacred Scripture itself is revealing to us that there are actions of Jesus not recorded in the Bible. Furthermore, Scripture also tells us that what is involved is not simply a few unrecorded events but a great many, so many in fact that what is unrecorded actually outnumbers what has been written down.

Finally, these unrecorded events must have a certain importance. Jesus would hardly have wasted so much time on unimportant matters. In addition, St. John is going out of his way to emphasize the unrecorded. The sentence quoted above is literally the last one in John's Gospel. As any author realizes, the last sentence of a book can be of tremendous significance since it contains the thought that will be uppermost in the mind of the readers as they finish his work. As he ends his gospel, St. John wants the followers of Christ to be fully aware that Jesus did a great many things that are not written down.

Historically, the Church has often used the word "tradition" to include those truths that were handed down from Christ but not written down in the Scriptures. In its Dogmatic Constitution on Divine Revelation, the Second Vatican writes as follows about the importance of both Scripture and Tradition:

> Sacred Tradition and Sacred Scripture, then, are bound closely together, and communicate one with the other. For both of them, flowing out from the same divine well-spirng, come together in some fashion to form one thing, and move towards the same goal. Sacred Scripture is the speech of God as it is put down in writing under the breath of the Holy Spirit. And Tradition transmits in its entirety the Word of God which has been entrusted to the apostles by Christ the Lord and the Holy Spirit. It transmits it to the successors of the apostles so that, enlightened by the Spirit of truth, they may faithfully preserve, expound, and spread it abroad by their preaching. Thus it comes about that the Church does not draw her certainty about all revealed truths from the holy Scriptures alone. Hence, both Scripture and Tradition must be accepted and honored with equal feelings of devotion and reverence.

Based upon St. John's Gospel and upon the historical teaching of the Church, a Catholic would be quite justified in believing that a doctrine such as the Immaculate Conception was known expressly by the Church from the Aposotlic Age but was contained in Tradition rather than in Scripture. On the other hand, a Catholic could also believe in the "implicit" explanation. Under this theory, a doctrine such as the Immaculate Conception is actually contained in Scripture itself—but implicitly—just as the mailman's statement about the cake revealed implicitly that he had met the husband. Furthermore, under the "implicit theory" it is even possible for a considerable period of time to pass before the Church, under the influence of the Holy Spirit, achieves explicit knowledge of a doctrine that was always present implicitly.

As applied to the Immaculate Conception, a Catholic who believed in the implicit theory of Revelation would begin by stressing that Sacred Scripture clearly reveals the special holiness of Mary and her unique role in the mission of Jesus. This is explicitly present from the very beginning. The Immaculate Conception is a doctrine that applies these two expressly revealed truths to a particular moment in Mary's life, the first moment of her existence. In other words, the dogma of the Immaculate Conception answers this question: Was Mary always holy in God's eyes or was there a moment when Our lady was not in the state of grace?

According to the advocates of the implicit theory, a considerable period of time could have passed before the followers of Christ began to ask themselves this question. They always knew about Our Lady's holiness, but at first they did not wonder about the first moment of Mary's existence.

Eventually, however, the question was raised. Then there was another long period of time in which the Church, under the guidance of the Holy Spirit, studied this question. Many of the Catholic laity felt instinctively that Jesus would never have allowed His Mother to be created in a state of sin. There must have been a close unity between Mother and Son from the very first moment.

On the other hand, a number of learned theologians took the opposite view. These theologians rejected the instinct of the faithful because they felt it was important to stress the truth that Our Lord had saved all men. If Mary were holy from the first moment, these theologians argued, then Our Lady could not have been redeemed by Her Son.

As has happened many times in the history of the Church, the instinct of the "unlearned" faithful turned out to be right and the reasoning of the "learned" theologians turned out to be wrong. The mistake of the theologians was twofold. First, if we consider their argument carefully, they were actually saying that for the great glory of Jesus it was necessary that Mary be born in a state of separation from God. When we reflect upon the great love of Our Lord for His Mother, it is not surprising that the Church eventually decided that such reasoning was inaccurate.

The second mistake of the theologians was to presume that they were as smart as Christ. Because the theologians themselves were unable to think of a way to reconcile the Immaculate Conception with the doctrine of Christ's universal redemption, they assumed that Our Lord could not think of a way.

Of course, not all theologians made such a mistaken assumption. In fact, there was a second group of theologians who strongly defended Our Lady's Immaculate Conception. In their discussions with the first group, the pro-Immaculate Conception theologians demonstrated that it was not only possible for God to reconcile the Immaculate Conception with Christ's universal redemption but it was even possible for the reasoning of men to do so. As one theologian pointed out, there are two ways to "save" a person from a mud puddle. The first way is to pull the person out after he has fallen in. The second way is to reach out your hand and prevent the person from falling into the puddle in the first place. Mary was redeemed by Jesus in this second way. (This is called "preservative redemption.") Just as it is possible to save a person from falling into a puddle, so it was possible for Our Lord to save His Mother from falling into original sin.

In summary, the implicit theory holds that the Immaculate Conception is truly revealed by God in what the Scripture tell us about Mary's holiness and special mission. However, the doctrine itself becomes known only in the course of time as the Church arrives at a deeper understanding of the revelation of Jesus. In contrast, the explicit theory holds that the Immaculate Conception is a truth known clearly by Christians from the beginning but contained in Tradition rather than in Scripture. Despite this difference, the implicit and explicit theories share much in common, particularly, the following three important beliefs:

First, that all the doctrines of the Catholic faith have been revealed by God and that this Revelation ended with the Apostolic Age. Second, that the Church can make great advances through the centuries in her understanding of what Jesus has revealed. (Even those who advocate the explicit theory can and do hold this view since, although they believe that the doctrines themselves were all known from the beginning, they also believe that the Church can develop in her appreciation of the meaning of these doctrines, just as the individual Catholic who reads the Gospels daily may advance in his appreciation of the words of Jesus even though he had read the same passage many times before.) Third, that the Holy Spirit guides the Pope and the bishops in the Church's understanding of Revelation.

One reason we have considerd the explicit and implicit theories of development in some detail is to prepare loyal Catholics for yet another trick of the dissenters. When faced with a Church teaching that they wish to deny, the dissenters will often attempt to undermine the doctrine by claiming that it did not exist until a certain period in history. Similar to the way that a good poker player attempts to bluff his opponents out of the game, the dissenters will look you in the eye and say with great assurance: "After all, that doctrine was only taught for the first time in the 11th century." Apparently the dissenters believe that such statements will devastate the faith of loyal Catholics and establish the right of critics of the Pope to do whatever they want.

An understanding of the proper role of Church development can help you to respond to this ploy. In addition, three other things can be said. First, since Church dissenters are usually propagandists for their own views rather than objective historians, one should never accept uncritically the truth of their claims. Second, many dissenters also call into question Church beliefs (e.g., the Divinity and Resurrection of Jesus) that were taught expliclty from the earliest ages and that have been the cornerstone of the Church's faith for two thousand years. In other words, the "historical" argument is not the real reason for the rejection of Church doctrines by such dissenters but is simply a public relations device in the attempt to destroy the confidence that Catholics have in the official Church. Third, despite their self-confident claims, the dissenters actually have no way of knowing that a particular Church doctrine "was only taught for the first time in the 11th century." What St. John the Apostle said about Scripture and Tradition is also true of the Church's written records in every age. The things that are written down make up only a fraction of what is actually taught. (As an illustration we could consider ourselves. Each of us knows a great many things. How many of these things have we written down? If we were to die tomorrow, would not most of us have recorded in written form only a small fraction of our total thoughts and beliefs?)

But even if Church dissenters were not manipulating the facts for their own purposes, even if they could somehow prove their claims that a par- ticular Church doctrine was "not taught until the 11th century," there would be no cause for alarm. All it would mean is that the implicit theory of develop- ment is the correct one and that under the guidance of the Holy Spirit, a doctrine that was always present implicilty in the Revelation of Jesus came to be known explicitly over a period of time.

The same Holy Spirit who guides the Church in her development can help us as individuals to remain loyal to the Church's traditional teaching. If we pray each day to the Holy Spirit for assistance, we can be confident of receiving the grace to resist the efforts of the dissenters to undermine our faith. May the following prayer always be on our lips, especially in moments of temptation:

"O Holy Spirit, in these days of doubt, confusion and uncertainty, come into our hearts with your light, your strength and your consolation. Come with the light of truth and teach us the will of God in our daily living, especial- ly now when God's basic laws are challenged or ignored."

7.
The Faithful, The Theologians, and the Magisterium

The last chapter, on the the development of doctrine, began with a quotation from Vatican II. Let us look at this quotation again in order to answer the following question: What are the three ways by which the Church can grow in her understanding of God's Word?

> The Tradition that comes from the apostles makes progress in the Church, with the help of the Holy Spirit. There is a growth in insight into the realities and words that are being passed on. This comes about in various ways. It comes through the contemplation and study of believers who ponder these things in their hearts (cf. Lk. 2:19 and 51). It comes from the intimate sense of spiritual realities which they experience. And it comes from the preaching of those who have received, along with their right of succession in the episcopate, the sure charism of truth. Thus, as the centuries go by, the Church is always advancing towards the plenitude of divine truth, until eventually the words of God are fulfilled in her . . .
>
> But the task of giving an authentic interpretation of the Word of God, whether in its written form or in the form of Tradition, has been entrusted to the living teaching office of the Church alone. Its authority in this matter is exercised in the name of Jesus Christ. Yet this Magisterium is not superior to the Word of God, but is its servant. It teaches only what has been handed on to it. At the divine command and with the help of the Holy Spirit, it listens to this devotedly, guards it with dedication and expounds it faithfully. All that it proposes for belief as being divinely revealed is drawn from this single deposit of faith.
>
> Dogmatic Constitution, Vatican II (On Divine Revelation, Chapter II)

According to the Church, therefore, a true development in understanding takes place through:

(a) the contemplation and study of believers (the role of the theologian)

(b) the intimate sense of spiritual realities experienced by those who are living their faith (the role of the faithful)

(c) the preaching of those who have received, along with their right of succession in the episcopate, the sure charism of truth (the role of the magisterium).

As the Second part of the Vatican quotation makes clear, Our Lord has given to the magisterium alone the crucial authority to decide whether a particular interpretation of Scripture or Tradition is legitimate, or whether, on the other hand, it represents a departure from the Word of God. As the Church has taught explicitly in other quotations cited earlier in this book, this special role of the magisterium means that the Holy Father (either acting alone or, if he wishes, in unison with his fellow bishops) can make doctrinal decisions that are binding in conscience upon all Catholics.

Keeping the role of the magisterium in mind let us now consider the special contributions that can be made by the faithful and the theologians, and let us begin by looking at the difference between these two groups.

As the very name "faithful" suggests, the faithful are those Catholics who have loyalty to the Church and her teaching, those Catholics who are "full of faith." The faithful live their religion and practice it with love in their daily lives. A theologian, on the other hand, is a person who is studying the faith, usually in an organized way. Theology has been defined as "faith seeking understanding."

A Theologian Must Be Faithful

In considering the role of the theologian, it is easy to overlook the word "faith" and remember only the word "understanding." The phrase "he's a theologian" can become the religious equivalent of "he's an intellectual." We think of a person who operates in an academic environment, somebody who teaches at a university and who has fifteen degreees in the subject, somebody who knows a thousand facts that we do not.

That can be one aspect of the theologians' role, but it is only a secondary aspect. As the quotation from the Vatican Council emphasizes, theologians must be first and foremost "believers who ponder these things in their hearts." The Vatican Council takes these words from the second chapter of Luke's Gospel where we are told on two different occasions (the Birth of Our Lord and His visit to the Temple when He was twelve) that Mary "stored up all these things in her heart and pondered them."

In other words, Our Blessed Lady was the first Christian theologian and, for that matter, the best theologian who has ever existed or will exist. Mary loved Jesus with all her heart. That made her "faithful." But Mary also did something else. For the Blessed Virgin, it was not only a total effort from the heart but a total effort from the mind as well. Mary employed all her intellectual abilities in a constant attempt to deepen her understanding of God's Revelation. That made her a "theologian."

Today there are many who call themselves "theologians" but who are not loyal to the Pope and to Catholic doctrine. Sometimes these individuals even hold positions of influence in what are supposed to be Catholic universities or Catholic religious education programs. Unsuspecting students come to their classes in the belief that they will learn about Catholic doctrine. Instead, these "theologians" use their positions to ridicule and undermine the official teaching of the Church. Their only loyalty is to their own ideas and, if their pet ideas are in conflict with the Church, then they do everything in their power to persuade their students to reject the Church's view.

The basic problem with such individuals is not their intellectual activity but their pride. They have developed their heads but not their hearts. The true theologians, on the other hand, are loyal Catholics who are conscious of their own limitations and who willingly accept the Church's judgment about their work. Their desire is to use the learning and intellectual talent they possess to help the Church in her constant effort to deepen her appreciation of what Jesus has done for us.

When their learning is joined to humility and loyalty, theologians can make an enormous contribution to the Church. Over and over again, for example, the Church has publicly acknowledged her debt to individuals such as St. Augustine, a theologian of the 5th century, and St. Thomas Aquinas, a theologian of the 13th century.

Nevertheless, St. Thomas and St. Augustine would be the first to acknowledge that it would be easy for them to make mistakes. They would point out that theologians are often pioneers. Like a pioneer, a theologian is attempting to advance from an area that is known into an area that has not as yet been fully explored. By the very nature of the process, mistakes can be frequent.

It is at this point that the attitude of St. Augustine and St. Thomas differs so completely from the attitude of "theologians" who publicly challenge the Pope. If the Church were to advise St. Thomas that on a certain matter he was treading on unsafe ground, he would have no difficulty in accepting the Holy Father's judgment. If any conflict seemed to develop between his own opinion and the official view of the Church, St. Thomas would presume that the Church was right and he was wrong. Today's dissenting "theologians" presume exactly the opposite.

At the root of this attitude of the dissenting "theologians" is a temptation that often comes to those who are engaged in intellectual pursuit. How easy it is for such individuals to consider themselves superior to the "common man." Like the Pharisee in the Temple, the dissenting "theologian" says to himself: "I thank you, God, that I am not like the rest of Catholics. I am a modern theologian, and that means that I have been given a special insight into the divine mysteries. It is my responsibility to teach the other Catholics what Christianity is really all about. It is the responsibility of the other Cahtolics to listen to my wisdom and to carry out what I say."

From there it is only a short step to attack the Pope and the bishops if Church authorities attempt to guide the "theologians." "How dare the Pope and the bishops sit in judgment on my work. They are not competent to do so. Rather, it is we theologians who should be judging their activities. I must do everything in my power to create a situation in which Church authorities will no longer be able to restrict the activities of a theologian in any way. Then at last we will be truly free."

Such intellectual pride is not new. In fact, it is the oldest temptation known to man. In the Garden of Eden, Adam and Eve had only one restriction. They were not to eat the fruit of a certain tree. That restriction galled them. They must be totally unrestricted—free to follow their own judgment. And the devil tempted them by claiming that, if they ate the forbidden fruit, they would "be as gods, knowing good and evil." Once the restriction was removed, however, Paradise collapsed. In God's plan, the restriction was essential to the proper order. In the same way, once the "theologians" remove the restriction of the magisterium, the theological world becomes a shambles.

That is the reason I have put the word "theologian" in quotation marks when describing those who dissent from the official teaching of the Church. In other fields of knowledge, it is possible for a proud man to be proficient. Good astronomers can be proud men. Good chemists can be proud men. But good theologians cannot be proud men because God is the object of their study and the knowledge of God is not reached by those who reject the order that He has established.

In considering the pride of the "theologians," we have been looking at a situation in which the head is developed but not the heart. Many good Catholics have exactly the opposite problem. They have developed their hearts but not their heads. They love their religion deeply but rarely study it.

Such Catholics are far superior to the "theologian" because a person who develops only his heart is a committed Chrisitan while a person who develops only his head is not. Furthermore, Catholics ''of the heart'' often possess a kind of religious instinct that may frequently be more profound than the reasoning of the most learned theologians. We saw an example of this in the last chapter with respect to the Immaculate Conception.

A Catholic who has developed his heart but not his head can be compared to a talented musician who plays the piano beautifully but who has never learned how to read music. As intuitive musicians have an ''ear'' that makes up for their lack of intellectual knowledge, so the faithful have an ''ear'' for religious truth.

Nevertheless, the ideal is for Catholics to develp both their hearts and their heads and we can appreciate the reason for this if we follow through on the example of the musician. Intuitive pianists who operate only by ''ear'' will usually be inferior in two respects to pianists who have added intellectual knowledge of their innate talent. First, while purely intuitive musicians may themselves be as skillful as their intuitive-intellectual counterparts, they will usually find it much more difficult to teach others. They instinctively know the right thing to do but they cannot intellectualize about it, and this presents a major problem in communicating their knowledge to other people.

In the same way, Catholics ''of the heart'' will often consider themselves unequipped to teach Catholic doctrine to their children. Actually, they could easily become the best possible instructors of their sons and daughters, but, mistakenly believing that such knowledge is beyond them, they rely solely on the ''professional religious educators'' in their Catholic schools or parishes. That works out fine *if* the professional educators are loyal to the teaching of the Pope. If they are not, however, the faith of their children is undermined rather than reinforced. It was to this problem of unloyal ''Catholic educators'' that Archibshop Fulton Sheen was referring when he made the following statement in 1972: ''I tell my relatives and friends with college age children to send them to secular colleges where they will have to fight for their faith, rather than to Catholic colleges where it will be taken from them.'' (Cf. *The Crisis of Authority*, Monsignor George A. Kelly, p. 98)

When the faith of their children has been undermined by the ''educators,'' or when they themselves read attacks on the Pope in their diocesan newspaper or encounter a dissenting ''theologian'' in their parish, Catholics of the heart usually feel very frustrated. They want to defend the Pope and Catholic doctrine—they instinctively know what is right—but, like the intuitive musician, their inabilty to intellectualize makes it difficult for them to communicate to others an effective defense of the faith.

In addition to the teaching aspect, there is a second problem facing the person who has developed his heart but not his head. By itself, an instinct (whether religious or musical) can easily be corrupted, especially if one is exposed to a great amount of trash. People with a fine sensitivity to good music can lose their "musical ear" if they are repeatedly forced to listen to junk. Similarly, the fine religious instinct of Catholics can be dulled or even lost if they are continually bombarded by "theological junk," unless these intuitive Catholics also possess a good intellectual knowledge of sound Catholic doctrine.

In summary, Catholics of the heart can become more effective in defending themselves, their children, and their Church if they also become Catholics of the head. How can this be done? By studying their faith under the guidance of orthodox theologians (*not* those who dissent), by reading books and periodicals that defend the Pope, and, most of all, by reflecting prayerfully upon the Bible, the official documents of the Church, and the speeches and writings of the Holy Father.

The Limitations of the "Expert"

"Theologians" and "Scripture scholars" who dissent from the Pope usually strive to create the impression that their rejection of official Church teaching is a result of their special knowledge, their "expertise." It is important for loyal Catholics to know that this is not the case.

To understand the limitations of any "expert," one must first distinguish between *questions of fact* and beliefs that involve a *value judgment* which is beyond the realm of empirical demonstration. Some beliefs do not involve value judgemnts and can be proved or disproved scientifically. Do you believe that the world is flat? Do you believe that Harry Truman was President of the United States in 1947? Who was the Pope in 1042? These are *questions of fact*. On such questions, the person who has done extensive research in a particular area (i.e., the "expert") will almost always have a factual knowledge that is superior to the non-expert.

On the other hand, our most important beliefs involve *judgments of value*, not questions of fact. Was Harry Truman a good President? Is Western democracy the best form of government? Is Milton the greatest poet in English literature? Or is Shakespeare superior? When, if ever, is it morally right to practice artificial contraception?

We need facts in order to make our value judgments. We have to know many things about Truman or Milton or artificial contraception. Nevertheless, even if we know all the facts in these areas—and we never do—that would be no guarantee that our decision is correct, because the most important part of our decision involves a judgment of quality. Furthermore, a person with a superior knowledge of facts is not necessarily a person with a superior value judgment. I may be an expert physicist while you are not, but your judgment about the value of our space program may be superior to mine. John may have greater factual knowledge about Milton than Peter has, but Peter may be a better judge of poetry. Harold, a non-expert, is no match for Warren, a theologian with forty-two degrees, when it comes to factual knowledge of Church doctrine. On the other hand, when it comes to judging the truth or value of a Church doctrine, Harold's judgment may be better than Warrren's, and it almost certainly will be if Warren is suffering from the spiritual disease of "theological pride."

What is being said here about the Church "experts" who dissent from the Pope is the same thing that was said many years ago about the Supreme Court by Justices Felix Frankfurter and Charles Evans Hughes. With respect to Court decisions, Justice Frankfurter pointed out that there was a great difference between the reality and the carefully created illusion, between what was actually happening and what the public was led to believe was happening. To quote Justice Frankfurter directly:

> People have been taught to believe that when the Supreme Court speaks it is not they who speak but the Constitution, whereas, of course, in so many vital cases, it is *they* who speak and *not* the Constitution. And I verily believe that that is what the country needs most to understand.

In a similar vein, Chief Justice Charles Evans Hughes commented: "At the constitutional level where we work, ninety percent of any decision is emotional. The rational part of us supplies the reasons for supporting our predilections."

Dissenting Church "experts" operate in the same way. Like the American people of Frankfurter's time, many Catholics have been led to believe that "theological dissent" arises from the expertise of the dissenters, their research and special knowledge. In reality, their "dissent" comes from their emotions. It has nothing to do with learning. It has nothing to do with expertise in theology or Scripture. Like Charles Evans Hughes, the "rational part" of Church dissenters only comes into play after their decision to reject Church teaching has already been made. It is at this later stage that the special knowledge of the dissenters is employed in an attempt to find "reasons" to justify what they already decided they want to do.

One way to demonstrate this truth clearly is to consider the past record of those "experts" who, in the years after Vatican II, began the public "theological" revolt against Church doctrine. In virtually every case, the dissenting "experts" had in previous years been quite vocal in defending the very teaching they now ridiculed. Therefore, if one assumes that their dissent comes from the intellectual expertise, one is faced with this puzzling question: Were the dissenters for all those years stupid when they accepted the orthodox Catholic doctrines? If so, how did they suddenly develop "expertise?"

It might be suggested that, during their loyal years, the dissenters were not engaged in the serious "theological" study that they now claim justifies their dissent. However, a look at their history shows that such is not the case. In their loyal period, they wrote books on doctrine, lectured at universities, and were considered "theological experts." Many even had the same theological degrees they now possess. Nor was their "loyal period" a brief and passing stage. Depending upon their age, many had been loyal theological experts for twenty or thirty years.

So the question remains. Were the dissenters stupid for all those years when they saw no conflict between their theological expertise and the official teaching of the Church?

Could their shifts in attitude be explained by some remarkable new factual discovery that persuaded the once-loyal theologians to become dissenters? Perhaps an archeological excavation in Mesopotamia unearthed startling documents that turned the theological world on its head? No, there was no such scientific breakthrough— no dramatic intellectual leap forward.

The truth is that the change from loyal "expert" to dissenting "expert" had nothing to do with intellectual factors. It was first and foremost a change of values. It was a shift from humility to pride, from reverence for the Pope to defiance. It was not a shift from ignorance to intelligence.

Once people have abandoned their previous faith, they often feel a psychological need to ridicule and sneer at those who remain faithful. An ex-Catholic frequently becomes an anti-Catholic. The dissenting "theologians" are no exception to this phenomenon. Ironically, one of the ways they attempt to discredit the Church is to claim (falsely) that Church doctrine has undergone a radical change. To "prove" this, they often go back seven or eight hundred years and quote statements out of context. If the situation were not so serious, there would be something comical in all this, for nobody has undergone a more radical change than the dissenting "experts" themselves. In their case, it is not necessary to go back eight hundred years. In their case, it is not necessary to manipulate the evidence and quote out of context. Only a few years ago they proclaimed the very beliefs that they now dismiss as incredible.

In summary, loyal Catholics should never be intimidated by the statements of "theological experts" who dissent from the Holy Father. In virtually every case, their statements have nothing to do with their so-called "expertise" but reflect their personal value judgments.

For example, if you have been following the attacks of the dissenters against Church doctrine, these statements will probably be familiar to you:

(1) "Theological experts" reject the Church's position on birth control

(2) "Theological experts" question Papal infalliblity and the doctrine of Mary's Immaculate Conception. "Experts" claim such beliefs are a hindrance to Christian unity.

(3) "Theological experts" express the view that Christ did not know He was God.

These statements, and hundreds of similar comments by dissenting "experts," simply reflect a private value judgment that has nothing to do with learning. If you chose ten people at random from your local phone book, their value judgments on these matters would be as good as those of the "experts."

Before leaving this topic, let us note again the pride and arrogance that permeate most of the statements of the dissenters. Consider, for example, statement number 3 that was quoted above. It comes from a number of "theological experts" who claim to believe that Christ was God but then go on to insist that Our Lord Himself was not aware of His Divinity during His Life on earth. If you think about it, these "experts" are actually saying that they know more about Our Lord than Jesus Himself did. Poor Christ! If only He had been given the opportunity to attend the theological courses of these experts! Then they could have advanced His knowledge to their own level and told Him of His true identity.

In discussing Church "experts" who have revolted against the Pope, we should always keep in mind the presence of other theologians who continue to be loyal to the Holy Father and to the official teaching of the Church. These are the true theologians, and they are often hated by the dissenters precisely because they remain faithful.

A major goal of those attacking the Pope is to diminish the influence of the loyal theologians as much as possible. In places where the dissenters hold power, they frequently employ their power to ban true theologians. For example, in our present topsy-turvy world, it is not unusual to find a "Catholic" university in which the religious-education program is largely under the control of people who reject Church teaching. At such universities, the loyal theologians are simply not invited to teach and, if they are already present on the facutly, efforts are sometimes made to remove them. In the same way, a diocesan newspaper edited by a dissenter will carry two or three weekly columns by "experts" rejecting the Pope while not "having the space" for even one column by a loyal theologian.

Ironic, isn't it? Censorship and thought-control practiced by the very people who champion the "right to dissent." Their position could be summarized as follows: "The Pope and the bishops must never use their institutional power to silence us, even if we reject Church teaching, but, on the other hand, it is perfectly legitimate for us to employ whatever institutional power we possess to silence those who disagree with us and who support the Pope."

While such an attitude is obviously inconsistent, the dissenters have an excellent reason for this posture. Their whole strength depends upon propagating the myth that "intelligent Catholics" must agree with their position. Scholars who defend the Pope could easily expose the shallowness of this view, if they were given the opportunity. Then the influence of the dissenters would collapse like a house of cards. Therefore, the true theologians must be banned in order to preserve the carefully created illusion of the dissenters.

Although they have frequently had to suffer much for their loyalty to the Church's magisterium, the true theologians have persevered. Their scholarship can be of great assistance to the faithful in the present crisis. And, as they themselves support the faithful, so these theologians in turn need the prayers and the love of all Catholics who are loyal to the Holy Father.

Conclusion:
God May Be Calling You
to Save the Church

Early in this book, we considered the relationship between St. Peter and St. John. Peter was the first Pope, and John was obedient to him. John fully accepted Peter's authority. Nevertheless, it was John and not Peter who was inspired by the Holy Spirit to write a Gospel. Matthew, Mark, and Luke were similarly inspired, but not Peter, the Pope to whom the four Gospel-writers were subject.

What does all this signify? It means that—always in conformity to the Church's official teaching and never in opposition to it—certain Catholics may be given a special grace or talent (a "charism") that is to be employed for the good of the entire Church.

Consider the great saints of an earlier period: St. Francis, St. Dominic, St. Ignatius of Loyola. They used their intelligence and their initiative to found religious orders that were invaluable in defending the Church at a time of grave spiritual crisis. In the 20th century, consider the initiative of Mother Teresa of Calcutta. All of these inspirational figures were humble and obedient to Church authority, but obedience did not mean a lack of personal initiative. On the contrary, they used every talent they possessed to defend the Church.

Someone might say: "But we are not spiritual giants like the individuals you have cited." True, but the principle is the same. Each of us has been given certain talents by God. If we are willing, each of us can make a contribution. The Church will benefit tremendously if all loyal Catholics will use the abilities they possess to the full extent in defense of the Holy Father.

There have been times in the Church when the faithful have played an especially important role in safeguarding orthodox teaching. For instance, between the Council of Nicaea in 325 and the Council of Constantinople in 381, during a period when the episcopate was hopelessly divided and when some bishops were even influenced by heresy, the faith of the Catholic people remained generally unshakeable and caused the eventual triumph of orthodoxy.

The faith and the work of loyal Catholics are no less important today.

If this book has been of any assistance to you, will you respond by doing whatever you can to defend the Catholic faith? Your prayers, your sacrifices, your study, your public and active support of the Holy Father— these are valuable gifts that you can give to God's Church.

And, if at times you must endure the criticism of the "dissenters" because you stand up publicly for the Pope, then do not be dismayed but keep in mind the words of the Bible, the advice given to all loyal Catholics by the very first Pope, St. Peter:

> Beloved, do not be startled at the trial by fire that is taking place among you to prove you, as if something strange were happening to you: but in as far as you are partakers of the sufferings of Christ, rejoice that you may also rejoice with exultation in the revelation of his glory. If you are upbraided for the name of Christ, blessed will you be; because the honor, the glory and the power of God and his Spirit rest upon you. . . . But the God of all grace, who has called us unto his eternal glory in Christ Jesus, will himself, after we have suffered a little while, perfect, strengthen and establish us. To him is the dominion forever and ever. Amen.
>
> (1 Peter 4:12-15; 5:10-11)

Appendix:
Books that Support
the Teaching of the Church

It is important for Catholics who wish to defend the Holy Father to know about the many good books and periodicals that are presently available. As a brief list, here are two works in each of four categories—statements of the Holy Father himself, Catholic catechisms, books that describe the present situation in the American Church, and Catholic newspapers or periodicals that support the Pope.

I. Statements of the Holy Father Himself

Two periodicals which regularly publish in English the texts of important statements of the Church's Magisterium are:

a) *L'Osservatore Romano*, weekly English edition (Rome)

b) *The Pope Speaks* (Huntington, Ind., Our Sunday Visitor, Inc.)

II. Catholic catechisms

a) *The Catholic Catechism* by John A. Hardon, S.J. (Garden City, N.Y., Doubleday and Co., 1975)

b) *The Teaching of Christ: A Catholic Catechism for Adults*, Edited by Ronald Lawler, O.F.M. Cap., Donald Wuerl, and Thomas Lawler (Huntington, Ind., Our Sunday Visitor, Inc., 1976)

(For school children, the series of books published by the Daughters of St. Paul is highly recommended. The Daughters also publish many other works in support of Church teaching. Their address is 50 St. Paul's Avenue,

Jamaica Plain, Boston, Massachusetts 02130)

III. Books Describing the Situation in the American Church

a) *The Battle for the American Church* by Msgr. George A. Kelly (Garden City, N.Y., Doubleday and Co., 1975)
b)*The Crisis of Authority: John Paul II and the American Bishops* by Msgr. George A. Kelly (Chicago, Ill., Regnery Gateway Company, 1982)

IV. Catholic Newspapers or Magazines that Support the Pope

As of the writing of this book, the following two periodicals have been in the forefront of those defending the Pope's teaching:

a) *National Catholic Register* (Twin Circle Publishing Company, Inc., P.O. Box 25986, Los Angeles, California 90025)

b) *Homiletic and Pastoral Review* (Catholic Polls, Ins., 86 Riverside Drive, New York, N.Y. 10024)

It should be emphasized that the works cited are in no way intended to be a complete list. Many other authors have written eloquently in defense of the Church, but the books and periodicals referred to above are a good place for Catholics to start if they wish to study orthodox Catholic teaching.

In listing good Catholic reading, it is easy to forget that books written years and even centuries ago continue to be invaluable. Recognizing that the classic works of the past present a very different view of the Church than the one they wish to propagate, the current dissenters have worked hard to create the impression among Catholics that anything written years ago is probably "outdated" and thus of little value to read. In reality, the classics of the past are no more "outdated" to a Catholic who loves the Church than the 16th-century plays of Shakespeare are to a person who loves literature.

Therefore, Catholics who desire to support the Holy Father can benefit greatly from the theological works of Frank Sheed (e.g., *Theology and Sanity, To Know Christ Jesus*)—or the excellent three-volume *History of the Church* by Philip Hughes—or the defense of Christianity by writers such as G.K. Chesterton (*Orthodoxy, The Everlasting Man*). In addition to such doctrinal works, there is also the inspiring spiritual writing of the past (e.g. *The Imitation of Christ* by Thomas a Kempis, *The Introduction to the Devout Life*, by St. Francis de Sales, *True Devotion to the Blessed Virgin Mary* by St. Louis de Montfort).

Most of all, of course, Catholics should read the Bible regularly in a prayerful spirit, asking the Holy Spirit to strengthen our own faith and to help us to support the Pope in bringing the faith to others.

A final word of caution about books. Selecting a book is similar to selecting clothes. People prefer different styles. Thus, a work that inspires one Catholic may not appeal to another. If you find this to be the case with any of the Catholic authors above, then do not worry about it but simply look for loyal Catholic writers that you find helpful. As there are many mansions in God's house, as there are many canonized saints from which we can select our special patrons, so there are many fine Catholic writers from which we can choose those who speak to us in the most effective way.